# Secrets Of The Shaman

# Other Controversial Titles From New Falcon Publications

*Undoing Yourself With Energized Meditation*
*Secrets of Western Tantra*
*The Tree of Lies*
    All By Christopher S. Hyatt, Ph.D.
*The Enochian World of Aleister Crowley*
    By Aleister Crowley, L. M. DuQuette, and C. S. Hyatt
*The Way of The Secret Lover*
    By Christopher S. Hyatt , Ph.D. and Lon M. DuQuette
*Aleister Crowley's Illustrated Goetia: Sexual Evocation*
    By C. S. Hyatt, L. M. DuQuette and D. Wilson
*Taboo: The Ecstacy of Evil—*
    *The Psychopathology of Sex and Religion*
    By C. S. Hyatt, L. M. DuQuette and G. Ford
*Pacts With The Devil*
    By S. J. Black and Christopher. S. Hyatt, Ph.D.
*Urban Voodoo*
    By Christopher. S. Hyatt, Ph.D. and S. J. Black
*Equinox of the Gods*
*Eight Lectures on Yoga*
*Gems From the Equinox*
*Little Essays Toward Truth*
*Heart of the Master*
    All By Aleister Crowley
*The Shaman Warrior*
    By Gini Graham Scott, Ph.D.
*Neuropolitique*
*Info-Psychology*
    Both By Timothy Leary, Ph.D.
*Zen Without Zen Masters*
*A Handful of Zen*
    Both By Camden Benares
*The Complete Golden Dawn System of Magic*
*What You Should Know About The Golden Dawn*
*Healing Energy, Prayer and Relaxation*
    All By Israel Regardie

And to get your free catalog of *all* of our titles, write to:

**NEW FALCON PUBLICATIONS**
Catalog Dept.
655 East Thunderbird
PHOENIX, AZ 85022 U.S.A.

# Secrets Of The Shaman

By
Gini Graham Scott, Ph. D.

1993
NEW FALCON PUBLICATIONS
PHOENIX, ARIZONA U.S.A.

International Standard Book Number: 1-56184-023-8
Library of Congress Catalog Card Number: 91-60063


First Edition 1993

NEW FALCON PUBLICATIONS
655 East Thunderbird
Phoenix, Arizona 85022 U.S.A.
(602) 246-3546

# Table of Contents

# CHAPTER ONE

## *NEW BEGINNINGS*

It was time to continue my training. My studies with the shaman master Michael Fairwell had thus far yielded *The Shaman Warrior* (Falcon Press, 1988), and two workshops I had developed. The workshops, based on the teachings, taught others how to apply these techniques to everyday life. One had just been published as *Shamanism For Everyone*; the other, *Shamanism and Personal Mastery* would be out next year.

Further, events in my life were leading to their own conclusions, and I was free to move on to something more. I had finished many projects: my book concerning a trip to the Soviet Union (*The Open Door: Traveling In The U.S.S.R.*); the birth of a game called *Glasnost: The Game Of Soviet-American Peace And Diplomacy* (both since published in the U.S.S.R., too); an experimental project which combined visualization techniques and shaman journeying (*Journeying The Shaman Way*); and most importantly, my fifth semester at law school. With three weeks at my disposal, I wanted something different to pursue.

A few months earlier, Michael had suggested I come to Los Angeles to continue my training, indicating my ability and potential to move up at least one or more levels. The group would have an intensive program prepared for my semester break. Such a prospect sounded very inviting, and I agreed to it.

"It will be a chance to achieve a level of mastery received by very few," Michael had told me. "We believe in your ability, and we have chosen you to share our message with others."

About a week before I was to leave, I received a schedule of activities, a map of the area, and a list of things to bring. The group had obtained a hotel room for me that was near the beach, but planned activities would take us out to other areas as well. The list of necessary articles included a power object (I packed

7

the long, black staff I had worked with before, as well as my black shirt), a small, framed 9"x12" mirror, a small crystal, and some photographs depicting a pleasant or empowering scene, such as the mountains and a forest. I didn't forget my typewriter or camping equipment, either.

I set out on December 16th, planning to arrive in L.A. some six hours later. The possibility of delays due to storms had been relayed to me, but I drove as if protected, and arrived within the time frame I had set for myself. I found my hotel without trouble, and within a few minutes time I had checked in and was met by Michael and another ODF member, Paul.

We went over my schedule during dinner. I would have two free days a week, but was to continue exercising even on those days in order to stimulate my psychic centers. I asked them why the group had left San Francisco.

"We left because we sensed the end of a cycle," Michael explained, "and felt our teaching work completed. We had linked up with other groups and had learned what we could from them, but we realized it was time to return to our home base, and incorporate all we had absorbed into a new teaching. The visit revitalized our work."

"What do you mean by revitalized?" I asked. "What kind of changes occurred?"

"Well, one was a deeper understanding of the feminine principle," Michael replied. "We met with many people involved with the Goddess religion, and we feel that shamanism can benefit from this central idea. For example, focusing on our earth as the mother lends itself to the respect needed for the planet in these times. Our understanding of the spiritual connections gathers our attention to honor and protect the mother of us all.

"Although Shamanism is itself non-denominational, it is a method or approach that has been linked with many religious beliefs, and it can work equally well with any one. Yet, at the same time, when you are practicing, it's important to maintain your own tradition, to know your own roots, and to use your own symbols. By doing so, you render those symbols that much more powerful."

"So how do you see yourself now?" I asked.

Michael looked thoughtful. "Well, we've drawn from many different traditions, but primarily we see ourselves as a Eurasian school, combining Western European techniques and Oriental teachings."

I mentioned that I had recently attended a shamanic workshop that used drums and chants in the tradition of the American Indian, and that many people I knew were involved with that aspect.

"We do not teach specific Native American practices," said Michael, "though we do draw on similar ideas that are shared by them as well as all shamans. For example, shamans all over the world share the notion of everyone on earth as all one people. This is a common belief, even though shamans are not in contact with one another."

"What other common beliefs do they have?" I asked.

"Well, the use of the laying on of hands for healing; the use of seeing exercises to get in touch with the spirit world; the common belief that the earth is the Mother and symbolized by the Feminine principle."

"And why do they all share these same basic beliefs?" I continued.

"Because there are certain universal principles when working with energy and contacting the spiritual forces. But beyond that the symbols themselves can differ, so people can choose their own paths in working with the divine."

Michael gave some examples of the sources of the symbols the ODF had chosen to work with. "For example," he explained, "we use the pentagram which is an eastern symbol; our work with mirrors and the Tarot are European. Breathing techniques are associated with India. We use gateways to cross from the everyday to the spirit world. American Indians do, too, because it is another universal. The only major difference between cultures is the type of gateway drawn. In any case, that's one of the things you'll be able to do soon—draw your own."

I then wondered about the people I had worked with in San Francisco and had written about in my earlier book *The Shaman Warrior*. Where were they now?

Michael explained that most had moved on. "And that's expected. We see our role as awakening the individual and his talent. We give them some tools and set them on the path. Basically, if someone follows the teachings through the 10th degree, they have achieved a high level of mastery and have gained all that we can give. Any additional work is on their own."

Paul cut in. "If you choose, you can continue to work with the group, though technically you are on your own." He explained that he was now past the 10th degree himself, but had chosen to stay on with the group as a teacher. "You see," he added, "we want people to find their own path. That is what is beneficial. But those who want can teach others, as I have chosen to do."

"The reason for this approach," Michael added, "is that each person's relation to power is individual. Each finds a personal, ultimate goal of achieving unification and oneness with the universe. Once achieved, a great sense of personal freedom and liberation is received. That's what the 10th degree is all about, achieving that ultimate freedom through this feeling of unity and connection. Then, with this personal power, we encourage people to go out on the road of life carrying this philosophy in their hearts, and applying the skills they have learned for success in everyday life."

"And after the 10th?" I inquired. "Is there anymore?"

"Oh yes," said Michael. "Some people go on quests to seek and work with power. I do that. Paul does that. But now you're getting ahead of yourself. You are at the 4th degree and should concentrate on the next two. There's no need to think about advanced degrees until you are ready."

Michael described what had occurred in the two years since I had worked with him before. He had stayed in touch with small groups he founded, and he now had about a half dozen personal students. He continued work on his own mastery, and was planning a trip to sacred power sites in the Middle East. Paul was working on his music, and was now teaching for the group. He had passed the 12th degree and would be assisting me in my training.

"So, now you are ready to resume your training," Michael told me. "What you wrote about in your last book was very basic training. Now, we will be introducing you to the intermediate degrees and a little of the advanced. Essentially, we will work on refining your skills for more mastery and power. To begin with, we will introduce you to the Elemental Kings, who are more powerful than the elements you worked with before. Are you ready?"

I said I was.

"Then let's begin."

# CHAPTER TWO

## *LEARNING ABOUT THE ELEMENTAL KINGS*

"Do you remember how we worked with the four elements?" Michael asked me.

I answered in the affirmative and recalled when we went out into the field and called on the four elements of nature—earth, air, fire, and water. I remembered some of the exercises we used to flow with the elements and to evoke their response. For example, there was the time that Michael and Serge had stood atop a high promontory, raising and lowering their staffs to flow with the currents of the wind, to get the wind to rise and die down in harmony with the staff movements. Another time Teri had called upon the spirits of the earth, and literally blended with them as she moved about in the moonlit night, shifting her shape to become a rock, a wolf, a panther, and then herself once more. Also, I remembered the time I had worked with fire. Holding my staff aloft, I had tried to feel the movement of the flames, moving my staff with the rhythm of the flames. Once, we had gone to the ocean, where Michael had us experiment with drawing the water closer to us, and with seeing misty elemental shapes rise up out of the water and hover on the horizon. In my own workshops described in *Shamanism For Everyone*, and in *Shamanism For Personal Mastery* I taught one to call upon the forces of nature to empower oneself.

"Yes, I remember our work with the elementals," I said.

"Well," said Michael, "our work was just a step. Now you are ready to engage in this work in a more refined way. Elementals are the spirits or energies of nature, describing a wide range of beings—from a large, hulking humanoid-like form beside a tree, to small, luminous ones that you might notice if you looked

closely under a rock. We divide the elementals into four
classifications in order to simplify our perceptions. Each is
associated with a traditional symbol. Earth relates to home life,
harvest, and the crops. Some people have used the earth elementals as guardians of the hearth. Fire connects with action,
power, and destruction. Water is associated with feelings and
emotions, and may be used in matters of the heart. Finally, air,
is traditionally linked with the intellect and the sending of
messages.

"On a higher level, however, each elemental corresponds to a
level of our consciousness. When we become more aware of
this connection, we see ourselves as a part of this elemental
kingdom, for we too are made of spirit. Through ritual and
training, we learn more of our own essential energy, and of our
power to mobilize and control those elements within."

I pointed out that I had used this visualization of the elements
in my classes to help people achieve various goals.

"Yes, that is what I mean," Michael replied. "But it is only a
step, for beyond the elementals, there are more complex forms
of energy. These Elemental Kings and Queens involve a higher
level of mastery over your own consciousness. But this new
level of development necessitates passage through a gateway.

"We can use an example to help us imagine how this is
achieved. In the Western system of Magic, the Qabalah, this
gateway is called the *Abramelin Magic*, named after Abramelin
the Mage, a Hebrew mystic who perfected a system of prayer
and meditation. After a period of intense meditation and
focusing, the individual goes out into the desert or to a confined
magical space. He will experience the passage through this
gateway when he senses intense unity with the divine in the
form of his own Holy Guardian Angel. An experience of the
Holy perfume occurs, and through this comes a direct
perception of the Divine creative force."

"Smelling?" I said puzzled, since I usually associated smells
with everyday earthly things.

Paul cut in. "Yes, you are smelling the divine. This scent
brings an intense knowledge of the good at the same time you
see the light. This sweet essence is unlike any perfume here on
earth, it is so pure. And through it, you come to new realiza-

tions. For that brief moment, you are at one with the universe, returning to what you have always known. The experience is very powerful and there is no mistaking the fact that you have crossed the line and are in the presence of the divine."

"That's right," Michael added. "It is a very powerful experience. Shamans all over the world use the gateway passage as a graduation exercise. The particular symbolic or theological content is up to the operator, based upon his or her own interpretation of the divine. But the results are the same—that intense sense of connection and knowledge of the divine."

I asked Michael if he could describe this experience.

"Well, you feel you are in the presence of someone or something that is understanding and forgiving, and at the same time, the experience can be horribly truthful. You are laid bare and must face what you see inside yourself. For some this may mean they make changes for the better. But then," Michael paused and looked at me darkly, "you must realize that for a few, the experience of truth is overwhelming, and it has driven them mad. This work can be dangerous. But if you are careful, if you have a good teacher, if you take it in stages and keep it in balance with the rest of your life, you should not have any trouble. So, are you ready to go on?" Michael asked me. "I hope I haven't scared you too much."

"No," I responded. "I'm ready. Keep going. I want to hear more."

Michael went on. "Well, in the Magic of Abramelin, once the Magician crossed the barrier, he conducted a series of evocations of very high beings of light and darkness. These may be compared to the spirits or archangels of Judeo-Christian systems. In any case, we work very similarly with high beings which represent the more advanced and refined forms of the elemental forces, and we call these the Elemental Kings and Queens. They are at the very top of the elemental hierarchy, and we work with both their lighter and darker aspects."

"Why their darker aspects?" I asked. "I thought you emphasized the positive purposes of doing this work."

"Of course," answered Michael. "We do. But it is also important to recognize these darker aspects in order to be truly balanced in your power. You will have the opportunity to do this while you are here."

"But why?" I wondered. "Why work with the dark? Why can't you just recognize that it exists and leave it alone?"

"Because," Michael responded, "the power itself is neutral. People employ power for good or bad purposes, depending upon their intentions. In this real world of good and evil, one develops the ability to work with power along the path, and must be exposed to both sides. In order to defend oneself, one must also know how to attack. That is why we believe it to be quite valid to teach these powerful techniques, even though they can be misused. We count on the student's moral fiber to use them correctly and with understanding. We know also that the power used in a negative manner will eventually return in a harmful way to the operator. You need to know the opposites in order to keep them in balance. Your control, your balancing point, will come from the heart. Your actions will be guided by this pure will. You will remain ever alert and sensitive to others, and your action will be determined by the actions of others, even if this means drawing upon your dark side to oppose a dark force.

"Realize also that as you advance, you may face some very powerful and intelligent forces. With this danger in mind, you will want to develop yourself psychically. Probably, a shaman who is less than an 8th or 9th degree in training could not do this. It takes a great deal of control and training to be able to go through this gateway and then work with these powerful energies. But, once you gain this power, working with such forces will lead to even higher levels of mastery. For example, you will be able to work with dragons."

"Dragons?" I said, puzzled.

"No, dragons are nothing like what you are thinking," he told me. "Rather, it is an amalgam of energies or forces, a little like a spiritual guide, but even more sophisticated and powerful. It is a very high angelic form."

Michael took out a napkin and drew on it with a pen to illustrate.

"One way to think of all this," he said as he drew, "is to think of pure light, the essence of the divine, at the very top of a pyramid of Beingness. Slightly below this are aspects of the divine. Further down, we encounter the angelic forms, or dragons, which partake very deeply of this divinity. Below them are the Elemental Kings and Queens, which you will learn to work with. And finally, at the base of this pyramid, are the elementals, the spiritual or energy forms representing aspects of the material world.

"However," Michael cautioned me, "it is important to realize that what I have shown you is only one particular pathway to the divine essence. There are many other forms out there in the spiritual world—spirits, ghosts, all sorts of things. You could choose from any number of forms to make a connection with the divine. However, the basic principles for achieving mastery are the same in other shamanic systems. The key is to choose the symbols or path that works for you, and then continue working on your mastery."

"How high can one go?" I asked.

"Well, that's hard to say," said Michael. "Like any type of education, one can continually discover new information. But basically, we designate the 10th level as a graduate. After that, the individual is ready to work on their own, creating their own path to higher achievement. To symbolize this, graduates will choose their own personal symbol."

Paul showed me the circular gold pin on the collar of his black ODF shirt to illustrate.

Then Michael cut the conversation short. "Anyway, we're getting way ahead of ourselves. It's important to start the training from where you are now. This will just give you a taste of what is to come. For now, we'll work on what you need to advance to the next level. And to start, I want to show you your daily exercise. This is something you can practice everyday to help open up your psychic centers and get the energy flowing."

We got up from the table, paid our bill, and proceeded upstairs to my room. I perched on the side of the bed, while Michael and Paul pulled up two wicker chairs.

"Now," Michael began, "the objective of this exercise is to stimulate your pineal gland, or third eye, which is the center of your psychic energy. You must awaken it, and it will be necessary for this intensive period of study. Do this as a daily meditation, a few minutes a day. Sit in a comfortable position..." I planted my feet firmly on the floor, and held my palms up in my lap. "Relax... breathe evenly. It's best if you close your eyes."

I did so for perhaps a minute, and heard Michael's voice go on in a soft monotone.

"Now you want to put energy out of your power hand—your right hand if you are right-handed. Hold up your first two fingers and imagine energy streaming out of them. Experience that energy coming to a point... You might think of this as a laser beam projecting out from you..." As I visualized the beam, I felt my hand tingle with a rush of energy.

"Then, bring the tip of this energy just above your eyes, pointing towards the middle of your forehead." I slowly lifted my hand until it was about a foot from my forehead. "Now slowly bring that closer to your forehead, but don't touch it. As you do, be aware that you are also putting energy out from your third eye, and notice any sensation."

I moved my hand a few inches closer, but stopped when I felt a sense of pressure, and reported this aloud.

"Good," said Michael. "That's common. It's like you are pressing a little knot of energy. When you feel this, pull your hand away, restart from the original position, but this time move your hand a little closer. After you repeat it a few times, your hand will be very close to your forehead, but don't touch it. Then, draw your hand back and bring it back again in a spiralling motion, like zeroing in on a bullseye. Keep repeating it in this fashion."

I repeated the movements while Michael explained more. "It's best to keep your eyes closed all the while. The sensation you feel is the interaction of the two energy fields, and the movement inward increases the intensity because of the powerful energy you are projecting from the third eye.

"Even after you stop the exercise, you will be able to sense energy when your hand is held further out, because now you have awakened the psychic center, and you will be more sensitive to the approach of an energy field. Repetition of the exercise will increase your sensitivity. Keep in mind that this is a healthful practice. You are stimulating your overall energy and are helping it to flow more freely. Like bringing more oxygen to all parts of the body, this is a great way to energize yourself.

"You should start each day this way as part of your daily meditation. Spend about ten minutes in meditation. Find a tranquil place for yourself, relax, focus yourself, and feel your energy and the energy around you. Incorporate your Third Eye exercise here. This exercise will help your work over the next few weeks."

As Michael and Paul got up to go, I mentioned that I was still feeling a tingling sensation in my hands.

"Well, that's good," Michael said. "You will feel this for awhile, but the main thing is to pay attention to the sensations between the eyes, since that is the center of the psychic energy. You can project energy from your hands, but then, pick up that energy with your head, so you notice the blending and interaction of these two energies."

I promised to practice this, and we set up our lesson for the next night.

"You'll learn how to really breathe, and how to move energy with your body," Michael informed me. "It's also a basic key to the rest of the work we will do."

# CHAPTER THREE

## *LEARNING ABOUT BREATHING THE SHAMAN'S WAY*

I practiced the psychic center meditation Michael had taught me in the morning, and then spent the next few hours exploring the Santa Monica beach. As I walked along the pier to the water, I felt very aware of the energy around me, even though there were few people about that day. Those few hours held a special sense of supercharged aliveness.

I worked the afternoon on the book, and after dinner, I journeyed high up in the Beverly Hills to begin the next lesson at Michael's house. When I arrived shortly after six p.m., I found Paul and his girlfriend Sara already there. They were seated around a coffee table in the living room. The huge bay window was shrouded with heavy curtains, and on the table had been placed assorted ritual paraphernalia—a cup, an *athame* or ritual knife, a censor, and a small bowl of salt.

Sara, like Paul, was in her twenties. She was dressed in a black shirt and dark pants, as was Michael and myself.

Michael, standing, began the evening. "Let's get started. We like to begin with a brief ritual. It helps to focus the energy of the group by creating a circle. Besides, the circle lends itself to the learning process."

At Michael's request, Sara dimmed the lights and rejoined the group. Michael picked up the small bowl of salt and made a circuit of the room with it. He then did the same with the silver chalice which contained some water. Picking up the burning incense holder, he walked around the room again three times in a clockwise direction. Finally, using his ritual knife, he drew four pentagrams in the air in each direction, and called upon the associated elementals to assist in focusing the energy and protecting the circle.

Now, the ritual over, Sara turned up the lights again.

"You may use any kind of ritual," Michael observed. "We start in the East since that is the direction of the rising sun. What is important is the creation of a circle with a strong protective focus."

Michael began the lesson with a simple meditation and a short astral projection to assist us in feeling the power of the mind more intensely, and to direct and control all aspects of ourselves. When the lights were dimmed once more, Michael directed us in the astral projection, and led us up above the housetops of the city. "Now you are rising up through the roof... Feel yourself rising and then gliding down the street as you see the lights of the city below... You notice the air, the birds, you are seeing the energies in the atmosphere move around." I could feel myself flying, and as I looked around, the energy in the air appeared bright, like gold flecks hit by the light and floating off into the darkness again.

I heard Michael's voice guiding us back. "As you approach, notice a cone of powerful energy coming up through the roof from the circle we created. Drop back into the center of this cone, and return to the living room." As we did so and focused once more on the scene in front of us, I felt the surge of energy emanating from the visualizations we had fashioned.

"Good, you are all back," Michael said. "And now I have something to loan you," he told me. He handed me a small white box which contained a gray slate of stone impressed with a raised oval shape with a series of striations running through it.

"This is a fossil of a trilobite," Michael informed me. "You can use this to do psychometry on an ancient object. As you work with it through your meditations, close your eyes and feel the emanations from it. They are from the time it was a living being. This should give you some interesting experiences of an ancient time."

I thanked him and confirmed I would use it. Then, he began the formal lesson by pointing to an outline shape of a human body with a line of seven colored circles that extended from the top of the head to the groin area. The bottom one was black; the one above it in the abdominal area was yellow; the solar plexus circle was red; the one in the center of the chest was purple; and the one in the throat area was green. Finally, there was a blue circle in the center of the head, and a white one just above the head.

"This is our interpretation of the chakras. In yoga there are twelve, but we work with the seven main centers. Work with these helps us to manifest and refine internal energies, so that we may raise and direct power. We distinguish between active and receptive chakras, and we seek to develop the more active ones to focus and project energy. In particular, the crown chakra at the top of the head, and the third eye in the middle of the forehead are used for psychic perception and intaking energy, while the throat and solar plexus chakras are points of energy projection. The bottom chakras are more static and may be used for storing power. They provide a center of equilibrium for the rest of the energy tree of the body.

"In fact," Michael went on, "these energy centers are just that, a focus for energy. As shamans, we perceive the body as a configuration of living, pulsing energy. Therefore, we interact physically and energetically with the environment. The body can viewed as a sensory organism, as well as a container for our being."

"How does this view affect the way you work with the body?" I wanted to know.

"It's very important," replied Michael. "Once we recognize this essential energy quality of the body, we can learn how to intake and project energy more efficiently. This contributes to better health and increased power at our command for the more advanced training we undertake, where circulation and focus of energy is critical."

Then, he turned to an explanation of one of the most basic controls for this energy—the use of breath.

"You will find the concern with the use of breath in many systems. In its spiritual, or mystical sense, the breath, or *Amhat*, is the central key for the movement of energy within and without the body, while breathing in the energy of the things around you yields the fullest sense of what's there."

I mentioned the sense of energy and aliveness I had felt earlier that day when I walked around the Santa Monica pier. "I seemed to be breathing in the sensations I felt as I walked around and observed everything so intensely."

"Yes, it's exactly that," said Michael. "You are literally becoming one with the environment around you through your breath. The physical act of breathing serves as a focus for the mystical act of breathing, leaving you with a strong impression of what you have just breathed in. Continual practice will provide increased power and vitality. This is central to your work in shamanism, and it is why we stress it so much.

"Besides the physical site for inhaling air, the human body has psychic sites also. The crown chakra and the third eye intake energy. Also, the solar plexus is a large center for exchange. In addition, although usually ignored, the soles of the feet are another center. The backs of the arms and forearms, and the hands are also important places. (Which is why it is best not to wear long sleeves). In fact, you may think of the whole aura as a sensory mechanism, with these few selected sites as being especially powerful.

"Most people have a core of energy which radiates out from the center as a living, radiant field. The field or aura has many channels in it and overlapping sections. This envelope is constantly changing, and at times there may be holes in it. This is why it is necessary to create an artificial circle around us for protection from those elements or sensations that we breath in.

"When one is trained, it is possible to view the state of a person's energy by observing the energy in the solar plexus. In a meditative state, it can be seen as a luminous ball at the solar plexus," he continued, as he drew a diagram of what looked like a squashed mushroom cap in a ball. You can even determine the condition of your own overall health and development by using a mirror. In this diagram, you can see the ball is like a mushroom which is folded in on itself. It has a short, central stalk, and then it blossoms out in a kind of umbrella of fibers, which link the core to the rest of the body. If the energy mass appears smooth and bright, it is a sign of vitality and well-being. You may see basic working colors of white, yellow, and blue. But, if there are dark masses or projecting spurs, this suggests problems in health or energy, since the flow is not smooth. An eruption in the energy ball may indicate that the energy is being drawn away, and could develop into a physical disease, which suggests a need to correct the problem as soon as possible."

Just then Paul broke in.

"You can also tell if someone has been hit by a psychic attack this way. Then you would see something more like a hole in the energy mass."

Michael went on. "You can learn about the development of the individual as well. As one learns to manipulate this body energy, the core will undergo a transformation. It extends and becomes less ball-like, looking more like a developed mushroom. This person shows some degree of skill which is not fully developed. In our system, he might be at about the fifth level."

Paul cut in again. "The more you advance, the greater your ability to focus this energy, and this is reflected in an increased skill in directing it towards a specific purpose, without the use of an external power object."

"There are numerous advantages to this more focused state," Michael continued. "A more focused core is more resistant to disruptions and disease. Your physical body will experience improved health as well."

He turned back to the series of diagrams and pointed to a third picture which illustrated an even more elongated mushroom-like shape. "As you can see, here the mushroom top has blossomed out even more, and there is a kind of astral spine under it, which contains an abundance of fibers. It's a little bit like a jelly fish made of luminous energy."

"But how do you see it?" I asked, while I attempted unsuccessfully to perceive these centers in their own solar plexus areas.

"The more you practice, the easier it is to see," said Paul. "It can also depend on the willingness of the person to allow you the view. The average person is not aware of even having this center, and so does nothing to conceal this. So he will wear it very openly. However, when someone is in training, he may want it to remain hidden, and it would be rude to attempt to perceive it.

"There are times, for instance in cases of healing or of understanding, that you can ask permission, if not in words, then on a psychic level. This indicates that in looking, you only want to help and mean no harm. Then, with this permission, their core will open to you and you can look. In fact, this process of perceiving the core involves an ethical consideration, since you are really seeing into the spiritual heart of someone. A shaman may accidently see such an energy core, but he probably has the permission to see or otherwise he would not have been able. It's a signal that you can come in, like an open door, while a closed door indicates you must knock or wait for the door to open."

"How can I see this?" I asked.

"Just be patient," Michael said. "It takes a specialized state of seeing. Initially, you'll start by seeing a glowing body of light at the energy center. Gradually, you will be able to see structures within it, but this takes time. You need to become a trained seer in a heightened state of consciousness to perceive these delicate energy structures. In any event, there is one last form you should be aware of." The drawing he pointed to looked a little like a squid with two long tentacles. "This image shows the energy drawn up into a thin column, like a closed umbrella shape. You may perceive it as a column or a flame. It develops as the individual is able to draw his energy up through the chakras until they are focused into a concentrated form. From this point, the individual can work great feats of power. It corresponds to about the tenth degree in our system, and it may take a few years, depending upon one's level of practice and commitment. When you refine this energy even more, it changes into a very fine point, like a thin tube that can be directed out like a laser beam to a particular end."

"Would I be able to see any differences in such a person?" I asked.

"No, not at all," Paul cut in. "Usually, such a highly developed person will shield himself, and will appear as an ordinary individual, even to another trained person. His core is protected so that others cannot look."

"In any case," Michael continued, "these exercises to develop the core are very important, in that it will affect your entire being, your whole energy field. As your core becomes more developed, you are more resistant to ill health; you have more stamina; you will eat less, and be drawn to better foods. Further, injuries will heal faster. And since mind and spirit are linked together with the body, you will experience greater mental alertness as well as heightened psychic awareness, because you are stimulating the energy flow in your body with this work."

On that note, Michael suggested a brief break. "When we come back, we'll talk about the major sources of energy you can use to stimulate and feed the energy in your own body, and some exercises to do so."

# CHAPTER FOUR

## *TAPPING INTO THE ENERGY SOURCES OF THE UNIVERSE*

When we returned from some coffee and sandwiches, we reformed our circle in the living room.

"I have a special energy-raising exercise to show you all now," Michael said. "It's a way of running energy through your chakras, using colors to assist you in visualizing what you want." As he spoke, he held up the outline of the human figure with the seven circles of color imposed upon the chakras, while Paul held up seven sheets of colored paper corresponding to these colors. You will use these colored papers to aid your visualization, but with practice, you won't need these additional tools."

Michael held up the black paper. "Now, get in a meditative position, and look at the first chakra at the base of the spine, which is associated with the lower pelvis, the anal and sexual centers. This is your base and your center of stability. Visualize yourself breathing in this black, solid energy, coming up through the base of your spine into this center. As you feel the energy there, place your hands into a linked position and hold them in front of this center. As you do so, experience this black, solid energy diffusing throughout your body."

Michael paused for a minute as we followed his instructions, and I felt a rush of warm, yet firm, energy move through my body, as if it were radiating from this lower point.

"Now, move to the next chakra in your abdomen; it's color is yellow. This time..." we all kept our eyes closed as Michael spoke, "see this yellow energy rising through the dark energy and becoming a yellowish light in your abdomen. Then, hold that vision..." we all moved our hands together in the same linked, holding position in front of our abdomens, "and see both the dark and yellow together. Hold this, and feel it diffuse."

Once again I felt another charge of energy going through me, although this time it seemed a little lighter, mixed with the heavier energy of before.

Now Michael instructed us to raise the energy to the next chakra, the solar plexus, associated with the color red. We had three colors to hold in our breathing. After feeling this color diffuse, we continued on to the purple of the lungs, thoracic cavity, and heart; the green of the throat chakra; and the blue of the third eye, or pineal gland. Michael continued the directions, "raise up the energy through the black, yellow, red... Let it blossom out as a purplish energy... Now hold this... Move on to the green...breathe it up...raise it up through the base... through the previous colors... See it gathering at your throat as a green luminescence... Then, hold...and experience it moving up and out."

Finally, we were at the last chakra. "Now as you breathe, bring this energy through the top of your head and out into space. Just let it out gradually. Keep it in an even column, and visualize it coming out, one step at a time. The sensation is like that of an inner core, and you may feel both a light-headed sensation and a definite feeling of your aura emanating out of the top of your head."

Michael asked us to repeat the process several times. "Just run the energy up the tree a number of times. Pull it up from the base through the colors to the top of the head. Experience that cord of energy running through you, feeling it's force and power."

It felt exhilarating and energizing to do this. After a few minutes, Michael invited us to return to everyday reality. Then, he had a few comments about the exercise.

"You will find this to be a powerful technique. You can use it as a self-diagnosis. If you sense weakness in any area, just place more energy into that area. At the same time, it can be used to focus upon any possible health problems which are developing by washing these areas with energy. Then, too, you can use this technique for balance. For example, if you feel light-headed, bring your energy down by focusing it back into the solar plexus. As the energy is compressed, use the black color to stabilize it. Use it likewise as a grounding method. Or, drawing red energy into and out of your solar plexus can be used as a powerful projection to accomplish some task."

I noticed Michael held his hands over his belly as he spoke.

"Why do you hold your hands there?" I asked.

"As a ground," he said. "It helps to move the energy up with your hands while you are doing this exercise. When you bring your hands together over any center, this helps to bring the energy tight, close into the body, by reinforcing your visualization. Also, it acts as a good shield against any external energy you don't want in there as you're pulling the energy you do want into your center.

"You should practice the color breathing exercise daily as part of your regular meditations. Doing so will increase your sensitivity of the other things you breathe in as well, and enhance your awareness. Using different colors is like consuming different energies, and you can learn to choose the type of energy you most need for a health or body need. You may find the color red holds a warming effect, while green can be calming and soothing." Michael held a few different colored sheets of paper in front of me to illustrate. As he held out the red and I passed my hand over it with my eyes closed, I felt a distinct warm tingle; when I did the same with the green, I a felt a sense of calm.

Michael put the paper aside and continued: "Further, you will discover which colors are the complement of your resonant colors. These complements are particularly energizing."

"How do I learn my resonant colors?" I asked.

"Just look at a strong light quickly. Then look away or turn the light off. Your resonant color is the first color you see." He held a small pen flashlight to my eye to illustrate. After a few flashes of this, I saw a faint purplish color.

"Well, that's your resonant color," Michael replied. "Normally, you will be grounded by your resonant color and energized by its complement. Some may find the opposite to be true. Breathing in different colors will teach each person their own truth. Using the colors can act as an aid to desired moods, and they are particularly helpful when expending a great deal of energy through shamanic work, since the ability to breathe in energy is as vital as air.

"If you were to go out into the woods or field to breathe in the energy from the plants and trees, for example, it's very important that you visualize the energy coming in as you breathe in. As you hold that breath, see the energy stabilizing. And as you breathe out, see the energy inside you dissipating and spreading throughout your body. Further, use the breathing to lend additional strength to your use of power objects by directing energy through your arm and hand. Breathing and visualization together are very harmonious and work to assist in the movement of energy."

"Or think of it this way," put in Paul. "As you take in energy, your breathing is a physical manifestation of that. It helps you to be harmonious and focused as you visualize that energy, and this visualization acts as a spiritual parallel to the physical act of breathing. You need to do them together."

Michael continued. "The sun and the moon are other energy sources, and are both very powerful and readily available. You can just drink in their emanations. You should hold out your hands and visualize the energy pouring into them and dispersing throughout your body as you breathe. With practice, you may eventually find that extending your hands is not necessary.

"There are many stories of yogis who claim to live off the sunlight and air, with practically no real nourishment at all. The sun relates to physical vitality, while the moon is associated more with energy level and psychic center regulation. Both are very energizing and can be used for either purpose." He paused to allow me some time to write all this down, as I had been doing all night.

"What about inanimate objects?" I asked. "Can they have energy too?"

"Yes," Michael answered. "But remember that as you bring in energy from your hands or feet, you are altering the central core. You can't continually act as a shaman without replenishing your source, unless you are so good that you can keep up the energy level automatically as you go along. Eventually, your channels will be so open and your body so accustomed to passing energy, that you won't need exercises to obtain energy. That point only comes with mastery.

"Now one last thing. You can also do psychometry with your breathing. When you interact with people, you are experiencing an exchange of energy. Taking in another's excess energy does no harm. As you breathe in the essence of a person or an object, you learn something. And the breathing in of energy can be used in shamanic healing. The healer breathes out the bad energy of individual, and replaces it with good energy of his own breath."

Michael had a quick breathing exercise to recommend to me. "Take a photo of a soothing scene, and breathe in the essence of the scene as a source of energy or relaxation. Or, you may find special times of the day in reality especially powerful for you. For example, if you see a beautiful sunset this may be a source of great power, or maybe there are other times, like dawn, that have a special resonance for you. Here, you are breathing in the power of the moment itself."

To demonstrate their words, Paul and Michael led us outside. We wore our coats against the windy night and assembled on the back lawn. As we stood on the patio, Paul stepped out onto the grass and extended his arms out while he gazed at the moon. As he did so, he appeared to blend into the darkness, although there was a shimmer of light, like a halo, flickering around him.

"What he is doing," explained Michael, "is gathering in some energy from the moon and the air around him. Then he will give us some of this energy, and we will practice drawing it in."

Paul moved his arms in an upward motion, then down, then up again.

"Now notice that he has made a connection with the moon," said Michael. Sara noticed it right away, but it took me awhile to recognize what she was seeing. What I saw appeared as a faint, fuzzy outline of a line, punctuated now and then by the clouds, projecting down towards Paul. Was I really seeing something, or just responding to the suggestions around me?

Michael was convinced of the truth of what I described. "That's the energy Paul is drawing on. When he extends his arms towards us, he is projecting some of that energy to us. You can draw upon this and sense its quality."

"Good, energizing," Sara said.

"I might say the same," I commented, although I still questioned whether it was just the brisk night air that made me feel so alert.

"This energy can be passed on to another person after you draw on it," Michael said.

Then, I noticed Paul moving around in a circle, producing broad, slashing strokes with his hands.

"What's he doing now?" I asked.

"He's building an energy structure, and he's using a visualization to assist him in doing so. He will use this structure to breathe in energy through it."

Now Paul appeared to be drawing his arms upward as if enclosing this structure and sealing it.

"The structure he's building is a pyramid. It's a way in which to take in energy. While you can draw it in with your body, say by taking it in through your hands or your solar plexus, visualizing a pyramid helps to intensify the focus, so one can build up even more energy."

Michael paused to allow us time to breathe in the night air and the energy being sent our way. I felt the essences of all the objects around us blending into one, and I paid close attention to my breathing. I definitely felt more vital and energized.

"Okay, from now on," he said, "breathing will be part of all of your work. Instead of just visualization, you must also use your breath to intensify your experiences."

We went back inside, and Michael gave me my homework assignment for the following days.

"You will do your pineal gland exercise for general stimulation, and then practice breathing in the colors through the chakras. Practice pulling them up starting at the base, then hold them in and feel the energy gather and disperse. Afterwards, ground the energy back down. Pay attention to any differences you sense in the environment, and to the quality of the experiences. Finally, make it a point to really breathe, and notice how you are bringing in and putting out the energy as you do."

As I drove back, I looked forward to the next day when I would practice my breathing by the ocean across from my hotel. And as I battled the highway traffic, I thought of several good reasons why shamans prefer nature over city environments.

# CHAPTER FIVE

## *LEARNING ABOUT PSYCHIC SELF-DEFENSE*

It was my third day of training in L.A. After I spent a few hours writing, I performed my psychic center and color chakras exercises, and then I headed out to the beach.

I spent some time experiencing the energies around me as I practiced my breathing. I sensed the frustrations of a poor man, the vitality of a group of runners, the eerie darkness under the pier. Feeling drained of energy from the gloom, I sensed a rush of warmth and vigor when I emerged into the rays of the setting sun, and breathed in the energy from the rolling waves and from the wind in my hair. I noticed a kind of stepped up energy as the sun went down—as if everything around me was hurrying up to capture the last of the daylight.

As darkness finally settled down on the beach, I returned to my hotel, leaving behind the experience of the beach and the last rays glowing on the horizon. It was time to go to the next class, which was to be on psychic self-defense.

I arrived that Sunday evening after six p.m., and met a new member of the group, Greta. Sara and Paul would not be there this night. Greta was a slim woman in her mid-20's, who worked as a paramedic.

Michael began the lesson with the usual ritual of creating the circle, and explained that it was used not only for focusing energy, but for protection.

"The circle is one of the most basic aspects of self-defense," he explained. "It's not just to focus your energy for whatever you're doing, but it is used to keep out unwanted influences that might be attracted by your work. These influences may be stray spirits, negative energies, projections from the curious, or those who are hostile or who disagree as to how one should conduct shamanism or magic. Your work, especially as it becomes more concentrated, is like a burning candle flame that attracts moths. Thus, taking some steps to protect yourself is a realistic precaution against the powerful energies and disruptions you may confront.

"You have to understand that the power you are learning to work with can be used for both good and evil. One real problem that many people have with magic or shamanism is that they may expect someone who has developed great powers will naturally wish to use those powers to manipulate others against their will. They may think that enlightenment is fine, but that the ability to harness the forces of nature is not to be trusted. Actually, the real key lies in the moral principles of the practitioner. Some may use these methods for perfectly good purposes; others to do harm. Therefore, it is necessary to develop rules and protections against those who might use these powers in harmful ways or against us. You need to be prepared for any unforeseen events."

"Isn't it difficult to tell where dangers are coming from?" Greta asked, noting that occasionally she got some hostile phone calls or letters from an unknown source.

"No, not at all," Michael responded. "Work on a psychic or magical level will always leave a personal signature. You merely need to tune into this signature, even if it is long distance. If you are sensitive, you can feel back psychically to the person who directed it by picking up on his willed energy. Only a very accomplished shaman or magician can work without leaving a trace."

"So what might you do in response if you pick up this kind of negativity directed against you?" I questioned.

"That depends on the situation," Michael replied. "One approach might be to mirror back the negativity to the sender. Eventually, as you become more in harmony with the universe, attacks will be less likely, but in the meantime, self-defense may be necessary.

"The kind of defense you use requires you to learn the character of the attacker and the different kinds of attacks possible. Realize that we do not believe in turning the other cheek. This will not work in the real world; therefore a true shaman must know both the light and the dark, even while he knows that the power itself is neutral. The factor that determines the nature of power is the person's heart. A true shaman should be of good heart, while keeping a defensive, receptive, open, calm, and relaxed nature to be responsive to the energies and feelings he experiences."

"How do you develop those qualities?" Greta wanted to know.

Michael answered, "If you don't feel you already possess these qualities, then act as if you have always had them. In time, your belief will create the reality you desire.

"When dealing with different situations, you will learn to become flexible and respond according to what your heart tells you. Approach with a good, yet receptive intention, and you will achieve a level of wisdom. If you are concerned about karma when you act, don't be. Your action is in relation to the other's action and in a sense, you are merely acting as a agent of a justified defeat. There will not be an accumulation of bad karma for you. Nothing should prevent you from acting in balance with what your heart tells you is right to do. Be ready to react with a good intent."

I wondered aloud about what types of things we might have to defend against.

"A psychic attack can take many forms," Michael said. "You might suddenly experience strange feelings of depression or anger with no apparent cause. You might notice unusual manifestations around you, such as strange noises or objects that move. Then, you might find things missing or turning up in odd places. Sickness or disease could be indications. All of these matters need to be approached with a clear head, and not assumed to be a psychic attack through a hasty conclusion. When odd things happen, they may be due to influences coming from outside yourself, but maybe not. So the key is to be aware and attune yourself to where these occurrences are really coming from.

"But how can you tell?" I asked.

"You can see this in the aura or the energy core. For example, you can determine a true attack if you observe holes, tears, or

discolorations in the aura. Another common type of attack manifests as nightmares resulting from the bad thoughts directed
against you, although it is rare that someone can control your
dreams. Another symptom might be a sudden psychosis or
madness, though this is also not a usual case. Still another
possible symptom might be the sudden loss of a job or a
disturbance in one's material well-being. Generally, a giveaway
that there is a psychic attack is when your material world is
suddenly affected by multiple difficulties.

"Of course, sometimes there can be perfectly natural causes
for such things; but perhaps not. Thus, to tell the difference,
when you are working with limited evidence of the cause,
remember to listen to your heart or inner voice, or to some
divination tool such as the Tarot. When you are sure of
yourself, it's up to you to determine what to do next."

I glanced at Michael skeptically, indicating my uncertainty
about whether such calamities might really be caused by a
psychic attack rather than just the chance manifestations of
everyday happenings.

"You can doubt if you will," Michael replied. "But disbelief
can be a person's greatest enemy. In fact, it's this disbelief that
contributes their true power to many negative sorcerers. If
intended harm is not believed, then no defense will be taken."

With this part of the discussion over, Michael turned to
specific techniques of attack. "As you work with and become
more sensitive to power and its many forms, you need to know
how to both attack and defend. I have with me a list of possible
attacks which we will go over first, since you must know about
the methods of attack in order to defend yourself against them.

"One of the most basic forms is 'negative overlooking.' An
example of this is when you wish another person bad luck or
simply think bad thoughts about them. You can do this in a light
or casual manner, or your thoughts could be more intense.
Realize that there are shades or levels of intensity, and when
negative energy is expended, it will have an effect. Our society
tends to discredit this view that there is a causal effect between
what one thinks and what happens. But the world constantly
bears out the effect of bad thoughts, and if someone is thinking

ill of you, you may experience some drain of energy or actual bad luck."

Michael drew a picture of an eye on the blackboard.

"The old-fashioned term for this is the evil-eye," he continued. "The idea is found in many cultures. For example," he picked up a necklace with large blue beads, and on each bead was an outline of an eyelike shape. "This is an example of a necklace used for protection against the evil eye. It's from Morocco, and it's blue because this is deemed a spiritual color which provides protection." He passed it to us for examination.

Then he passed around a small blue bowl with eyelike designs upon it. "You can find eyes as a protective motif on many objects. There is a long history of belief in the existence of the evil eye, which is based on the belief that through thoughts, one has the power to work ill on another. But then, how effective it is depends upon the other person's defensive awareness. If you seek to protect yourself through the eyes or through other measures, this can be an effective deterring measure.

"The next type of attack is actual spells. These may run the gamut from very simple curses to very complex spells, with all sorts of ritual trappings, including candles, incense, and mirrors. The basic principle of the spell is based upon the focus of will and power through the visualization of the intended victim. When he sends this focus as a spell, curse, or ritual, he in fact transmits a beam of negative energy to the person he intends to harm. The difference between this sort of attack and just wishing or thinking is the greater degree of focus, the greater investment of intention.

"Going on, we move to attacks through dreams. But this is rare, since it requires a specific and developed ability to enter another's dream.

"Fourth on our list are weapons using dolls or image magic. We find here a sophisticated and calculated spell, which uses a doll or an image of the intended victim as a focus. Although we usually think of this as a negative approach, the method can be used for positive ends also, such as in healing."

Michael paused for a moment, then continued. "Another, more sophisticated method of attack employs entities, such as negative familiars. The elemental is bound in service to someone, and is used to attack others. A traditional example is the witch who uses her cat or its spirit. Perhaps more common is a person sending out an image that results in a haunting by a negative entity. Usually, after a time, the sender will draw the entity back to himself after it has accomplished its harm."

I questioned the existence of this type of attack.

"Yes, the use of these familiars is quite true," answered Michael. "Although using them is rare because it requires a tremendous focus and ability, it is possible. You will have a chance to try this yourself. We will let you create your own familiar as proof."

For the next item, Michael drew a picture on the blackboard of a long, narrow projection that looked like a spear point.

"A sorcerer can also use energy darts and bone pointers as psychic attack weapons," he explained. "Both tools are probably the oldest magical weapons known to man." He moved his hands in a kind of circular motion in front of himself, as if he were molding a clay-like object in the air. "A magician would use motions like this to create an energy dart, since a dart is a visualized body of energy designed to function as a psychic bullet." Pulling his hands apart and slashing one hand through the area, it appeared as if he were breaking the dart he had created. Then he continued. "These darts are generally about 4 to 6 inches long, and a half inch wide. They are a very compact and concentrated form of energy, designed to penetrate any defense that may have been set up. Then, the dart will discharge its energy like an exploding bullet. Also, these darts may be used as a visualizing tool or exploratory device to penetrate into what is beyond."

"Could you explain the definition of gateways again?" I asked.

Michael explained briefly. "A gateway is an opening into another level of reality beyond the everyday plane. By sending an energy device in to see what it might be like in there, one can learn without having to go in there oneself, so there's less risk. Or one can use this method to explore before the ability to transmit oneself is developed."

Now Michael reached into a box beside him and pulled out a small, white piece of bone, perhaps the size of a chicken leg.

"Another psychic attack method uses the bone pointer. It's a traditional Australian aborigine technique, for example. The bone pointer is a power object that can send out an energy dart or a beam at the intended victim. However, unlike the energy dart created through visualization which I spoke of previously, this is a real object, and not just a visualization."

Next, he held up a small knife.

"Closely related are magical daggers. Tibetan sorcerers use these to send out negative energy to their victims. These weapons can inflict an immediate loss of energy or an injury, and they have been known to cause anything from long term disability or disease to death. The seriousness of the harm depends upon the seriousness of the intent. In all of these matters, the negative energy has a direct effect all alone, and it need not depend upon the victim's belief to have effect. You will have an opportunity to experience this for yourself later on when we work with sending out energy darts. Though, of course," Michael smiled "you'll just get a light taste of this."

Michael referred to his list again. "Now just two more types. Another subcategory of the hauntings we talked about earlier are poltergeist phenomena combined with a psychic attack. Here, there may be ghosts or negative energies that naturally gather around a negative person, yet they are initially inactive. An actual psychic attack can activate these energies to react against the individual they are surrounding.

"And finally, there are time traps. This involves the use of probable times in the future; therefore, this is a long range strategy. Essentially, one visualizes an event occurring in the future against someone else. Through constant re-visualization and reaffirmation, the event comes to pass.

"Suppose you become involved in an argument with someone at work. This person could then visualize you having a fight with someone else, such as your boss. The time trap has been set, and it may occur if it is reinforced with intense visualization. Also, such events work only if the factors necessary are already present in the environment. Sometimes people imagine intended bad situations without realizing that these negative things can come about.

"For all of these types of attacks, it is necessary to learn the shape of them in order to be prepared to defend. In very serious situations, you may find that your best defense is an offense, although this is a very dangerous action to undertake. If any of the things you send out bounce back, they can hurt you on a magical, psychic level. Keep in mind, however, that we are reviewing this topic merely because it is best to take precautions in this world. As your power grows, it deserves better and more advanced means of protection much like owning a nicer house or more expensive property can potentially attract more powerful attacks. Thus, enjoy that power for the benefits it brings, even while you take more precautions to protect yourself in its use.

"For example, there was a time when our group sensed an attack from someone of a different magical school. Some of us experienced financial problems or cars breaking down. When we realized what was happening, we put up protective shields around ourselves, and the problems stopped. In fact, later, we learned we had been right when another member of the group told us that this group member had been doing this."

Greta described a situation in which a woman owed her money but was refusing to pay. "I sent her a firm letter, and then I visualized myself arguing to a judge in a small claims court, if it came to that, and I saw the judge deciding in my favor. Shortly after this, she sent me the money."

"Good," said Michael. "Now that is a time trap. You were looking ahead and affirming in advance what will be. You were using it both offensively and defensively in that you were taking some positive action to get her to pay, while defending yourself against her refusal to pay. And you were successful because she paid."

Michael gave a few more examples of common everyday psychic attacks and defenses, drawing from experiences on the LA freeway.

"Even a simple bolt of energy can be very effective as either a block or an attack. For example, on the LA freeway there's a lot of aggression as people get frustrated with all the traffic. So one person, while driving will build up some negative energy and send it to someone else by giving them a look or the finger. And they may not even be aware they are doing some powerful psychic act in projecting this charge of strong negative energy.

"For instance, one member of our group was driving along the freeway when he suddenly saw a hot rod barrelling towards him with some rock music blaring loudly. At the last minute, my friend was able to pull out of the way, and as the hot rod zoomed by, he sent out a blast of hostile angry energy, with immediate results. Almost at once, the muffler on the hot rod split off, and the car skidded to a screaming halt in the middle of the freeway, and my friend drove on feeling much better, like justice had been done."

"But was it a coincidence?" I wondered.

Michael shook his head. "There are always alternate possibilities. But as you hear more and more of these stories, the evidence mounts up that these forces are real and have an effect."

"I have an example that might help convince you of the power of these energy forces. About ten years ago I worked at a print shop, under a mean supervisor who picked on everyone as a means of ensuring his position. One day we were working together on a limited run of printed invitations, and he was especially concerned that none should get mangled, since we had no extra stock for replacements. However, he was running the machine too fast for me to handle the folding of the invitations. When I asked him to slow down, he sped it up instead and yelled at me for being too slow. I realized that I could level the playing field by placing my hand on the machine, giving it a charge of energy, and sending out the thought 'Since he won't be reasonable, start eating these.'

"Almost at once, the machine jammed, and started spitting out the invitations like torn-up confetti. It was amazing. My supervisor panicked, and then his boss came out, very angry. When his boss said: 'Let me try,' I touched the machine again only this time I sent positive energy. The machine worked fine. I experimented once more after his boss left by successfully breaking and fixing the machine with my touch, and I had barely started to study about these things at the time. So you see that even machines possess a spirit that can respond to energy."

Michael moved on. "If you are going to launch a successful offense or defense, you need three things," he said while turning to a chart on the blackboard. It was a drawing of a triangle, upside down, with the words: *Ability*, *Will*, and *Knowledge* written along each edge.

"Essentially what this means," said Michael, "is that you need the will and power to use this energy we have been talking about. You need ability to send the energy out with the proper method of delivery. And you must acquire the knowledge of where to send it and what you do as an appropriate response to the situation. All three qualities are interrelated, for your knowledge impacts on your ability to act and helps you direct your will. In turn your ability influences your will and informs your knowledge."

"What sort of things do you need to know?" I inquired.

"You need to find the source of the negative energy, so you can respond properly. If you are sensitive enough, you will be able to pick up on the individual signature left behind. When you have sensed the source, you need the ability and receptive heart to work with this knowledge.

"What you might want to do is to psychometrize people as you meet them, using this information to aid in recognizing any future hostile sensations against you, which you may perceive. Further, upon making a new acquaintance, tune into who they are or where they are coming from. Alerted, you can take steps to avoid possible future problems, perhaps by evading interaction in the first place, or by holding shields in place when you meet. In other words, it might be that all you need to defuse a potentially difficult situation is not to give any energy to this person.

"Also you can use divination to discover the source of problems, perhaps through the use of mirrors, the Tarot, astral projection, or the I Ching. Just be careful not to let your imagination fill in details. This will come with training."

We took a brief break for coffee and cookies in the kitchen, and when we returned, Michael was ready to start on methods of defense.

"A common method of defense is a run of the mill energy shield. Here, people have set their minds and emotions in a solid closed position so they cannot be swayed. But this type of shield has absolutely no effect against psychic energy, and an attack will move right through this. What is needed is a visualized shield."

Michael went on to describe these types of shields.

"One type will provide around-the-clock protection, which you can easily engage through your breathing exercises. You create a more resistant aura, and you visualize your aura or energy field firming up around you as you breathe. Each time you breathe in, you might see a wall of energy moving in to hold a firm position around you. As you breathe out, visualize it pushing away outside negative energy.

"Another type of defense is the magical circle, the most basic tool to assist in focusing psychic energy and creating a defense as you perform a magical or shamanic working. You may draw this circle around you physically or mentally, then seal it closed against the outside energies.

"Pentagrams or other forms of geometric banishings can also provide a safeguard. Some might use a cross. The shape of the symbol depends on you and your background. You may draw it in the air with a power object, such as a staff or a knife, or you may draw it mentally. To create a complete shield, you should form it in all four directions around you. Some traditional shamans also draw it below them and above in order to seal all possible areas."

Michael then drew a picture of a circle around a car.

"Creating a portable circle is a way you can form a protective bubble around yourself as you move, perhaps as you are driving or flying in a plane. This can't prevent things entirely, but it can soften any possible problems, and it will provide a sense of safety if you are feeling nervous. To really boost the effect, you can augment the circle technique with a pentagram or other shape as we discussed.

"Here's an example. A few years ago, I worked on a security patrol, and found myself facing a potentially explosive situation. As I got out of the patrol car to confront some drunk and drugged out rowdy teenagers in front of a drug store, I placed a bubble of energy around myself. Then, I visualized a pentagram in front of myself to push them back. As I stepped forward, the group suddenly moved away and dispersed. I could actually see the energy pushing them back.

"Now, very often the energy you encounter may not be directed against you personally, but when you extend out this protective field, it makes them aware of your individual presence, and they back off."

For a few moments, Michael paused to rummage around in a box of magical objects, and then he continued.

"There is also the blue light method. In the face of some negative energy, you can project a soothing, blue light from the center of your third eye or pineal gland chakra to evaporate the negative energy. However, this technique is not very powerful, because it is very brief and only moves in one direction. Plus, if you just project light out at someone, without sufficiently controlling it, you may just end up giving him or her an energy charge, rather than deflecting and smoothing their negative energy. But as you develop the ability to visualize better, this technique will become more effective, and you can use it as a quick energy fix to turn something negative away, a little like a martial artist deflecting a blow with a quick flick of the wrist."

Michael now held up some of the small stones and flat discs he had removed from the box. "These are amulets and seals," he said. "These amulets can be any small object you've charged with a protective visualization. Or you can make or draw a seal with a certain magical intent, or design it to act in a certain way based upon what you visualize. For example," he held up the image of a five-pointed star, with some hieroglyphic-like symbols along the five points and the image of a small eye in the center, "this is a kind of all-purpose protective device. I've written some words of protection on each of the points, and then the eye acts as a general way of looking out for and warding off negative energy.

"A good way to use these objects is to carry one or more protective amulets with you, since you can't be alert at all times. These will act as a watchdog. They are not designed to ward off really sophisticated, organized psychic attacks, but they are good for regular day-to-day encounters with common, diffused hostilities of others' anxiety or frustrations. One might carry a seal drawing on a piece of paper or a metal disc either in their wallet, purse, or pockets." He handed me the piece of paper with the five-pointed star and the eye.

"Here, a gift for you," he said.

"What do these symbols mean?" I wondered. "And how should I use them?"

"You can use it much like any banishing protective object. The eye acts as a ward against any general negativity, as I mentioned before. The names I have written in the five sections are those of Elemental Kings and Queens I have encountered who have helped me in my work. In making this seal, I have invoked them to impart a large amount of power into this. You should find it very helpful. Just carry it with you, maybe glance at it from time to time, and charge it with your own energy for extra protection."

I thanked him and placed it in my wallet and put it away.

He continued down his list outlining a few more defenses. "Names also impart a great deal of power, so you can design your amulets, seals, and other objects with powerful names. The elemental workings you do will put you in contact with these spirits, and then you can build your own amulet, such as in the form of the star I just gave you. When you do this, it will be more effective than anything I can give you, because you will have invested it with your power, so it will respond to you best."

"What sort of powers should I invest it with?" I asked, as I had not yet worked with any of the Elemental Kings or Queens that Michael had used in energizing the star he gave me.

"It doesn't matter what names or spirits you use," he answered. "Choose names that hold a meaning for you. For now, you can fill it in with the names of the general elementals—earth, air, fire, and water, and with spirit overall. Charge the amulet as you would any power object, by focusing your attention, and imagine projecting energy at it from your eyes or your hands. By the same token, you could charge an amulet that has already been fashioned to serve a protective function. To illustrate, take out the seal I gave you." I brought it out and placed it on the table in front of me.

"To activate it, use a power object, such as your knife or your working hand, and trace over the design, injecting it with your power. As you draw, you charge it, and then you inscribe the names in the air with the tip of your power object, the knife here, or with your hand. If you were making your own seal, you could draw the concept of each element, and charge each fully with your magical intent. Then, once it's charged, keep the amulet or seal in your wallet or on your dashboard, or with you somehow. Also, it's a good idea to seal it in plastic, as it will last longer.

"A power gift from someone else can also be a good source of protection. That's because when you bestow a power gift on someone else, you are expressing real care, since this extends your wing of protection to them and it also links you karmically to some degree. As a result you will feel a disturbance yourself if they are hurt or injured." As I returned the seal to my wallet, I thanked him again, and with more feeling this time now that I understood more what his gift really meant.

"We will now move on to other means of defense," he said, "one being walls of force. In this case, you are mentally drawing a wall around yourself, keeping out the outside forces. Remember that all these choices of protection give you more options, so you can use what feels most appropriate or comfortable when you need to use something.

Such protections can also be used to help protect your home. You can protect your living space by placing charms, seals, shrines, or masks at strategic places, or by harnessing an entity to a particular object or area in your home. Then that protective energy will radiate from that spot and you can also call this energy forth in even greater strength when needed. Whatever defense you apply in your life, use what feels comfortable at the moment.

"Another way to deal with negative energy is to create a reflective or rubber form in your mind to bounce the energy back at the person, or you might visualize a mirror blasting it back. Generally this will work, although some power can be designed to cut though such devices. This protection is a matter of choice, as I realize that some people will be unwilling to purposely return harm to another. Don't use it if it doesn't feel right.

"Still another way is to form a gateway diversion. This is more advanced, but you can open up a hole in space to catch the negative energy, and then it gets absorbed into another dimension so it doesn't affect you. Or, as a basic general defense you can put up a cloud of energy around yourself. But this is only good for light uses; it will not stand up against a serious attack."

Michael glanced at his list once again. "Another defense for light use is to shoot a rainbow of colors at someone. This requires a lot of force to work, since a minimum effort could result in it easily being sent back at you.

"Then, too, you need to learn how to combat the psychic eye. As you grow in ability, there may be other individuals out there who project themselves astrally in order to observe you. If someone is doing this, you will sense being watched even though there is no one around. One way to deal with this is to simply paint the intruding eye shut with your mind's eye. Or you could open up a gateway, and let the eye look through there."

"It sounds like a dangerous psychic world out there," I observed.

Michael smiled reassuringly. "Yes, I know it may perhaps seem like that, and I know I have given you a lot to think about, but I don't want you to feel that you are taking on more dangers by working as a shaman. Despite all these precautions, you will find that as your strength and knowledge grows, you will need these protections less and less, and that it actually becomes safer out there in the psychic world. We are merely staying prepared, and others will sense this. If, however, you should ever become hit, and are suffering, you can use a means of self-healing, which we discuss at another time."

For now, Michael had a special demonstration to show us—how to make, use, and protect ourselves against the energy darts we had talked about earlier, and so, we repaired out to his backyard to do this.

# CHAPTER SIX

## *LEARNING HOW TO USE ENERGY DARTS*

"Now I'll show you how to make and work with energy darts," Michael said, and we put on our coats and went out into the brisk night air. There was about a three-quarters full moon and it lit up the backyard with a hazy glow.

Michael stepped onto the small triangular patch of grass beside the patio and motioned for me to join him. Greta stood nearby on the patio and watched.

"Okay," said Michael as I stood beside him, "now what you want to do is take your two hands and put them together with cupped palms facing each other, about six inches apart. Notice when you are doing this, you are projecting energy, and it will form between the hands as you will it." He demonstrated as he talked. "Slowly visualize the energy assuming a cylindrical form as you roll it with your hands and form a point at one end."

He squeezed his hands together slightly, and then held out his left hand palm up as if he were offering me a gift. "And here we have one," he exclaimed triumphantly.

I glanced at his hand and seemed to see a faint, whitish, fuzzy image. Greta observed from her vantage point, "Yes, that's a really firm one, I can see it."

Michael, turning to look at the end of the patch of grass, extended his left hand holding the dart, and placed his right hand behind it. "What I am doing is coming in with the palm of my right hand, and sending energy out of it to push and launch the dart." As he did so, he bent down to the area of projection on the lawn and slashed the point of contact with his hands.

"I had to destroy it before it went too far," he exclaimed, "since there is nothing out there to stop it. You don't want to leave these around, as the energy can last a long time and it could be harmful."

He returned to his position beside me. "I will repeat this. As I start rolling the dart, I put out energy and visualize the energy coming to a point. This time, however, I will only send it out a little ways, and just leave it hanging in midair. I want you to look at it," he said, while pointing to an area about ten feet in front of him. "Go ahead, just walk around it. See what you see, but don't get too close."

Greta appeared focused upon something, but I didn't see anything until I started circling around the designated area. As I did, I noticed the same white mistiness in front of me.

"Very solid isn't it?" proclaimed Michael. "If you look more closely, you may notice that this energy is bullet shaped." And indeed, it did appear a little like that.

"Okay," said Michael, "now I'll get rid of it. The easiest way is to form a banishing pentagram to destroy it." He zapped the air several times with his knife. "Now, it's gone."

Next, Michael wanted to show how these darts could be used in target shooting, and he asked Greta to step into the middle of the lawn. "I'll just be shooting at her energy, not at her," he explained. Then calling to her, he said, "I'd like you to give me a silhouette."

For a few minutes Greta stood there silently, her feet planted solidly apart, her hands by her sides. As she did, a whitish, fuzzy outline seemed to spread out around her.

"Notice that she is putting out a lot of energy. She is projecting this out about a foot." When she stepped back onto the patio, Michael continued, "She has now severed any connection to the field. This leaves a human silhouette of energy on the lawn. Use your seeing exercises to see it." I nodded that I thought I could see a hazy shape.

He then proceeded to form a dart once more, and pushed with his palm to fire it. He motioned me to move forward with him.

"Now you should be able to notice a change in the energy silhouette where the dart has entered. As it hangs there, it discharges energy into the target." I agreed I could perceive some sparks or flashes.

We stepped back and Michael shot another dart into the target. "In Australia the sorcerers actually fire into other people, but we are only demonstrating. Greta doesn't feel anything as she is not linked to the form anymore. It is just free floating energy." He took a few more shots and then tugged on my sleeve excitedly.

"Now notice how the figure has become more luminous. It has had six hits, so it's really boiling with energy. You must be especially careful when stepping up to it as it can discharge out up to ten feet. If you would step into it, you would be hit, and the negative energy would latch onto you. You might feel general distress, maybe headaches, maybe worse. In any case, it's something you want to avoid." And with that, he quickly slashed the area and finished with a sweeping motion as if he were pushing everything away with a brush.

Next, he stepped into the center of the lawn and formed his own silhouette, and then severed the link with it. He led me to this energy target and asked me to cup my hands and try to visualize the energy between them.

"See a column forming, and as you see it, roll it out, as if you were rolling a point."

I kneaded my hands back and forth for about a minute.

"Yes," Michael exclaimed. "There, you have a column of energy about six inches long and one-half inch across."

My experience wasn't quite as vivid, as I just noticed a fuzzy white form, although I felt a definite tingling sensation between my palms, and it felt like something with a bit of heaviness was between them.

"Now," Michael directed, "leave the dart in your left palm, bring your right hand behind it, and move it forward enough so that the heel of the right palm comes in contact with the energy field of the dart. Then, push, and picture the dart moving out into space."

I did so, and then looked ahead about fifteen feet to the spot where Michael had sent the previous darts.

"See," he pointed out, "It just took off, and there, it's hitting the target."

I saw a little spark of light ahead of me. Michael suggested I try a few more shots, and I practiced rolling and sending them off. When I was finished, he had a few tips for me.

"As you practice this, your focus will become more refined, and your control over the flight's direction and speed will improve. You need to hit it hard and fast, but not so hard that you destroy it, as this is fragile." Then he wanted me to destroy it.

"Go up to it, but not too close to stay out its radiation field. Then, make a banishing pentagram or other geometric form to banish it." I approached and stopped a few feet away. Then, as I drew the pentagram, Michael instructed me on my drawing technique, and asked me to broaden my strokes. He had me continue until there was nothing left. "And now, use a wiping motion to disperse the energy. Just brush it away, and that destroys it."

Next, he had me practice forming my own silhouette. Under his instruction, I stood with my eyes closed and palms outstretched. I visualized the energy forming around myself, summoned up the power inside me, and projected it out with each exhalation of my breathe. I spent a few minutes on this, and then Michael asked me to sense the energy becoming solid. Next, he had me run my hand up my back, over my head, and down my face and front of my body without disturbing the energy field, all the while visualizing the energy separating from it, as if I were cutting myself away. When I felt separated from this energy, I stepped away and out of the area.

After I returned to the patio, I observed what I had formed. I saw a kind of gauzy image that looked like the aura around someone's body, except that I could see the hazy outlines of the bushes behind it.

Michael motioned for me to make another energy dart, and I aimed it at the gauzy image. There appeared to be a slight dark spot in the air where I projected it.

"See, there's nothing to it," he exclaimed. "You didn't feel anything, did you?"

I shook my head.

"That's because the target is just energy. But you can notice the reddish area where the dart hit, and the bright flash in that area. That's caused by the interaction of the energy field of the dart and the field you left behind."

He went over and destroyed the field as before by making a few slashing banishing pentagrams with his knife, Then he paused a few moments to breathe deeply. When he returned, he explained that he had used a technique to recharge his energy after all that exercise.

Then Michael had a special surprise for me. "I'm going to fire an energy dart at you. Is that okay?"

I looked at him a little nervously. I wasn't sure I wanted to be hit by one of them.

"It will be alright," he assured me. "I'm not doing this to be malicious, but it's important that you become familiar with the sensation, in case you have it done to you by someone else. Then you will know what it is and what to do for it. By knowing what is happening, you can quickly put an energy shield up to ward off any further attacks."

I stepped out onto the lawn again, and watched as Michael rolled an energy dart.

"I'll tell you when the dart is coming," he called out. "I want you to receive it. Don't put up any shields against it. I'll remove the dart as soon as I'm done." I watched as he sent it towards me, and felt a slight pressure against my left shoulder, like a gust of wind blowing. I asked Michael to send one more while I kept my eyes shut, so I wouldn't be able to anticipate its arrival. A few moments later, I felt the same gentle gust of pressure in my chest, and I heard Michael cry out: "Now there. That was a hit at your chest. Did you feel anything?"

I described the gust of pressure as a kind of tingling.

"Good," said Michael, "and now, if you look down, you can see it sticking out of you."

I noticed a fuzzy flicker of something in front of me.

"Now, I'll put a little more energy into it," Michael continued, and I felt a bit more pressure. "That's because I can send energy through the dart into you. The dart has created an energy link which allows me to do this.

"And now," he said coming towards me, "I will pull the darts out." He made a few tugging motions with his hands and stepped back. "The area will be sensitive, since it has been ruptured. Use your breathing exercise, and hold your hands over the area, circulating the energy. It will heal, but you need to visualize it happening."

I focused on the energy circulating as he had instructed, and I soon felt a warming sensation through the area.

"That's fine. If you feel solid, as if your energy is all together and back to normal, fine. But if you feel any discomfort, repeat the exercise. It's important to heal the area, because hits of psychic energy can last a long time."

"Well, I really didn't feel that much of a hit," I said.

"And for a good reason," he explained. "When I sent the dart, I didn't want to hurt you, so it wasn't sent with a negative intent. It was sent as a focus of energy to give you a sense of what a hit might be like. Negative attacks are more intense.

"If you have a shield in place before the attack, such as a banishing pentagram, the dart will enter the shield instead of you and remain there."

Michael stepped into the center of the lawn to demonstate. "Now shoot a dart at me and I'll use a banishing pentagram in front of me as a shield. Then watch what happens.

I shot another dart, and when I said I couldn't see what happened to it, Michael pointed a few inches in front of his chest. "There it is." Then as I approached to look more closely, he asked me to notice a thin blue line in the center of the pentagram.

"That's he energy dart stuck in the pentagram. It's like putting on a bullet proof vest."

Then, after dispersing everything with a banishing pentagram, Michael demonstrated a few other shapes, observing that:

"Various geometric shapes and protective circles will work just as well. So if you should ever see one of these darts or other negative energy forms hurling at you, just quickly put up a protective shield, and it will catch the energy. You can then break the energy up or blast it with some of your own energy, and then it will no longer be negative and will only scatter. Of course, energy cannot disappear—it merely changes form and can always be re-gathered. Now, how would you like to learn to create your own energy shield?"

I nodded.

"Creating your own shield merely involves visualizing a circle of energy around you. Watch as I form one." As he stood in concentration, I noticed a slight glow of his aura around him.

"Notice how it just expands outward and wraps around, and how, when I take a few steps forward, you can see the hint of a band of light. This shield will last about twenty-four hours, unless I take it down. You can put it up at any time, and the average person won't be able to see it. But you must be specific in your visualization; if you are vague, such as just visualizing a blue light around you, then there will be too many holes and weak spots through which any negative energy can find it's way in to you."

"So how do you visualize it to protect yourself?" asked Greta.

"I just visualize a definite band of energy coming all around me and terminating in a full band or circle of light around my body. It's like a hula hoop, and it's just a waist band, not a full bubble. But its power extends upward and outward all around me."

Michael suggested I try to create one myself. I planted my feet firmly and tried to see the energy extending out of me. Meanwhile, Michael coached me. "Okay, take it slowly at first... That's right, draw it all the way around you... I just saw the energy curve around your arm... Now bring it around the small of your back... Now continue the energy back around so it encircles you... Once it has encircled you, visualize it as one solid and complete circle."

When I was finished, Michael tried taking a few shots at me. But I never felt the darts, and they just stayed stuck in the shield.

Then, Michael told me to banish the darts that were hanging in the air around me. "Just direct some banishing energy at them," he commented. "And don't worry, this won't destroy your circle, as it is a very strong and effective device. If you are going to go walking around with this for awhile, it's a good idea to visualize the energy encircling you from time to time so you strengthen the barrier. Like I'm doing now."

Michael made a circuit around the lawn and joined us back on the patio. He then explained other forms of energy projection.

"It doesn't matter if the energy is negative or positive. There are three basic forms. One is a simple ball of energy," he explained, "and although it's very typical, it's not very well formed." He threw one at us to demonstrate. "You see, the feeling is very slight as compared to the dart..." He threw one of these, "...which is much more precise. But it's more linear, and as you can see, it missed..." He glanced towards the other end of the patio. "You see. It's now sticking out there in the garden." He made a few motions to banish the energy ball and dart. "And finally, there's just an energy wave. Now notice how diffuse that is...and it disperses very quickly."

We experimented throwing around different types of energy, and then Michael explained the banishing process in a little more detail. He began by making a few of his usual slashing and thrusting motions in the air.

"Now you'll notice the spiralling motions I'm making," he said. "I'm forming the banishing pentagram. Five strokes to make the star, and then pow, I send it out. It's a very definite, solid blast of energy, and it shatters any concentration of energy, positive or negative, that has gathered there. But it could be any geometric shape. The important thing is to send out energy with an effective repelling force. You could visualize all of this with your eyes alone, but it's easier to do this physically. For example, look."

He gazed intently at Greta for a few moments. "I've been looking at her with an aggressive look, and her energy field has become agitated, so she has been putting out some energy herself. Here there is an energy exchange, and I'm not making any gestures or motions. It just has to do with the will. We're putting out energy all the time, and this can occur even without looking directly at someone. They can pick up on your energy and send it back."

Michael had one last way of working with energy to demonstrate—creating a gateway to direct or capture energy.

"You won't be ready to do this yet," said Michael, "but you'll find it pretty amazing. Look at our target," and he pointed to a small bush across the lawn. "I've created a small gateway in front of it. Watch what happens when I fire a little energy down the gateway at the target."

I watched, but didn't see anything, and told Michael.

"That's right," he exclaimed. "The energy goes right down the gateway and vanishes. Look more closely at the patch of space in front of the target. The gateway is still there, but the energy is gone."

I peered ahead straining to see something, as Michael made a few downward strokes with his hand in the air. As I watched a kind of gauzy translucent line seemed to vibrate in front of me.

Michael continued:

"You see, when I throw some energy at my target, the gateway intercepts, so the energy I projected disappears. It gets whittled down to a point of nothingness as it goes through the gateway.

"But then it reappears in another gateway somewhere else." Michael pointed up to a spot about 20 feet above us in the sky. "And there it is. It has appeared in another gateway, because of my ability to visualize and create gateways. I can have the energy come out at another spot by creating another gateway wherever I will. The principle of the gateway is to cut through the fabric of reality. It's a hole in space and time, and when some energy goes into a gateway, it goes from the real through a hole into someplace else."

"Someplace else?" I asked puzzled. "Where's that?"

"You'll learn more about that someplace else in the field," he said. "Although you may find it hard to understand, it's another space, like going into another dimension. It's like something out of science fiction, but it's real. When I create another gateway, the two are linked, because they exist simultaneously in space and time. Energy that enters the one, exits at the other. It doesn't curve around, because the end of the one gate is the beginning of the second, or the other way around. Also, remember, the energy was not stored anywhere in this reality."

"Like a time warp then?" I suggested.

"Yes, that's the general idea. We're not dealing with anything linear here. The energy is not moving from A to B to C and so forth. Rather, it's really going into A; then I open up Z, and there it is. There is no intervening travel. It's just there.

"You must keep the simultaneity of these gateways in mind when you are working with them. It's like the possibility of instantaneous movement from one part of space to another. Essentially, what this means is that you can move around in one reality without travelling much distance, and yet you can be at the other side of the galaxy at the same time. Incredible, isn't it?"

I nodded, not certain what else to say.

"Well, just think about all this," Michael said. "These ideas can challenge your everyday ideas about ordinary reality. We're working with altered states of consciousness and other dimensions, so you'll find that gateways are very important to our work. They become an everyday working tool, much like learning to see into other realities. And you'll soon learn that, too—how to use these as an everyday aid for transcending time and space. It isn't as spooky and weird as it may sound, and it's a means of gaining more personal power. Believe and you will see. Learn to enter gateways, and you will acquire the knowledge."

On that note, the evening's lesson ended. We went inside, and Michael reminded me to continue practicing my pineal and color breathing exercises. "Also, remember to take advantage of the energy of the sun and moon. Breathe in their energy and store it inside you. If you observe something powerful in the environment, breathe it in for general energy. This is all part of gathering power."

Also, Michael reminded me to keep in mind the defenses we had just studied. "You will be learning to open up a gateway very soon, and anything can come through, so you need your defenses together. It can be very risky without protection."

I wanted to understand the risks, but Michael preferred to go over this later on. "When you learn how to make a gateway, you'll be supervised, so you'll be safe," he assured me. "You will make a partial gateway, and step into it to experience the other dimension. Then you'll come back with what you have learned. That will earn you a grade if you can accomplish it."

But first, I had much to learn. Tomorrow, we would be going on a field trip to a natural history museum where I could practice my seeing and feeling. Then, I would spend more time learning about mirrors and gateways, before I would be ready to step into another dimension. Michael asked if I still wanted to try all this, even with the risks involved. I agreed that I wanted to go on.

"Good," said Michael. "Tomorrow we will visit the museum, and you'll have a chance to refine your abilities. Then I'll test you to see if you can really do it. Are you ready?"

I said I was.

# CHAPTER SEVEN

## *LEARNING TO SEE AND SENSE AT A MUSEUM*

Michael and Greta arrived shortly after ten at my hotel to take me to the museum. We were headed to the Los Angeles Museum of Natural History, which housed some of the oldest artifacts known to humans. We were interested in fossils from dinosaurs, pre-Columbian artifacts, and ancient Native American relics. Also, we would work with gemstones, minerals, and living fish.

"Essentially," Michael explained, "we are using our breathing or the palms of our hands to obtain a sensation of these things. These will be advanced psychometry techniques, and the goal is to breathe in and feel the essence by internalizing these objects and let any images come to mind. We will work together and singly, and compare our findings."

"What kind of information should we get?" I asked.

"Well, we want to get some information on the history and nature of the object, something concerning how and why it was made. Rely on your intuitions and feelings, and notice the images you receive. Later we will compare our observations to check our overall accuracy."

When we finally found our way to the huge stone complex in the middle of the city, and entered past the museum shop, the first thing Michael stopped at was a large horse-like skeleton. It had a long, thin skull, and it was splayed out on a simulated mud floor, as if it had died on the spot.

Michael felt this was a good example to start with, and he held out his hands and breathed deeply. Greta and I followed suit. He wanted us to get a sense of what it was like when the skeleton was alive, but I could only visualize the bones before me. I asked Michael what he was experiencing.

Michael moved his hands over the area several times and spoke slowly, with his eyes half-closed. "I'm picking up a kind of greenish color, perhaps of grassland. And now I'm seeing hot sunlight. There's brownish color along the ridge of his spine. The animal is up, loping gently, like a grassland kudu from Africa. It's sometime in the afternoon and it's summer." Michael continued the description and then said, "This is what I'd like you to do next time, without knowing anything about the animal. We can check the descriptions and gauge the accuracy."

We moved down the corridor and stopped in front of a case with a large, slightly greenish, cream-colored fish with a huge, projecting jaw called appropriately enough a megamouth.

"Don't read the description yet," Michael instructed, "and tell me what you get off this. Use your seeing and feeling exercises to sense the environment of this fish."

I tried to push logical conclusions aside, and let my eyes go out of focus as I held my hands over the case. As images came, I reported them. "I'm getting a sense of something deep and dark... I'm noticing some kind of volcanic tip of a mountain... It seems hot. I see the image of the sun, perhaps a feeling of warmth."

When I stopped, Michael appeared very pleased. "Good, that's a start." He pointed to the description above which indicated that this warm water fish had lived in an area of much volcanic activity. "You see, you did pick up essential things. And another key when you do this—look for irregularities that stand out. These represent things that are making a stronger impression on you, and so they are more likely to be accurate about whatever you are reading."

We walked on down the corridor, and Michael led us into a room devoted to pre-Columbian artifacts. We stopped in front of a case with small, hollow, clay figures, that looked a little like kneeling gargoyles, with their arms spread out like wings.

"You will find that human-made objects can be very powerful, even more so than the animals, since the objects have been invested with human intention and power. For example,"

Michael pointed to one of the figures before us, "these have a lot of energy stored in them. They were taken out at special times. I get a sense of priests, pyramids, and that it was brought out in a procession."

We moved on to the next case. "Now you try. Pick out an object that seems especially powerful."

I noticed one strange object, possibly a large urn, with the face of a man with bulging eyes, a scowling mouth, a long projecting nose, and large elephant-like ears that looked like handles.

As I held my hands over it, I could only sense priests holding the object in a procession, like a ritual.

"Well," Michael announced, "I get a sense of blood. It was an incense burner used in rituals having to do with bloodletting. Probably it had something to do with the sacrifice of war prisoners, because I can feel an aggressive, warlike energy. Try again."

I held my hands over it again, and now I did feel firmness or strength in the tingle of energy from it.

"You see," Michael exclaimed, "as you become more aware and pay closer attention, you do see something. I can feel the traces that the blood left in the suffering of the victims and in the power unleashed by the blood. But all this comes with training. You become very sensitive to extremely subtle vibrations of energy. Using symbols and images, you can translate those into events or activities."

We walked on past other things as Michael ran through the feelings he was picking up. He wasn't interested in having us match him with our guesses, but rather, he wanted us to really feel, and let go of rational perceptions, even if we saw somewhat differently among ourselves. It didn't matter if we were correct or not. What was important was to truly get in touch with our feelings and let the logical part of ourselves go.

Michael also reminded us to look past the scary appearance of some of the bizarre, oddly shaped objects we passed, which had images of strange long-beaked birds and some gargoyle-like images. "Some of these were used as funerary urns and household deities, or as watchers to ward off negative spirits. So don't be fooled by appearances. If you concentrate on your breathing and feeling, you'll really get a good feeling from them."

As we were about to leave the pre-Columbian exhibit, we came upon a large rock stela that had the image of a male figure standing erect, with some thick carved and curving lines, like snakes, emerging out of his head. It had an odd fascination about it, and we stood gazing at it for a minute or two, trying to sense its story.

"It seems like a vision from a drug trip," Greta said.

"It says it was a statue of a ball player," I said, reading the sign.

"No, no, it wasn't that," exclaimed Michael, suddenly rushing us away. When we regrouped in the hallway, he explained. "That was an incredibly powerful object, full of negative energy. As we were standing there, I suddenly felt my energy lowering, as if it was being pulled away by that statue. I felt a strong sense of blood sacrifice associated with it. In some of the old games, the captain of the winning team would be sacrificed. In any case, I suddenly felt my energy being drained, and felt we had to get away."

Greta also reported feeling weak. Michael suggested we head for the cafeteria to replenish the energy we lost. While we made our way there, I asked Michael why these stone objects could still house such energy after thousands of years.

Michael explained. "They still have an effect because they are not dead at all. Some of these objects have had or have spirits in them even now, and when we look at them, we may be reactivating those spirits or tapping into the original intention infused into them. Remember, too, that some were used in sacrifices, and the spirits are used to being fed. When someone sensitive comes by, they might seek their energy. Perhaps I felt it even more, since I'm more open and receptive to such energies."

I still had my doubts. Michael continued to explain. "Even though many years have past, these objects are charged, even as we charge our own power objects. Then, too, a shaman or magician might have caused a spirit to reside in it, and being an archaeological artifact, the entity is still there. Some objects are a source of great power, considering the fact that they may have been venerated and worshipped by people for centuries. That power can still linger today.

"The positive or negative energy could lie dormant for many years, but when someone with sensitivity comes by, it reactivates the energy, and you can almost feel it leap out at you, such as Greta and I felt with the stela. Now, this energy may be good or bad, depending what kind of magic was used with it. But you don't know in advance. So there can be some danger in opening yourself psychically to these old objects. If you pull in a lot of negative energy all at once, you could pull in something you'll regret. It pays to touch or feel these objects lightly at first to get an overall picture. If you sense any problem, just move away."

Michael related the story of Howard Carter and King Tut's tomb as an example of archaeologists coming in touch with negative energies.

"It's an old story and many people know it. After Carter opened up the tomb, a lot of bad luck followed all of the people on his expedition. A few died shortly thereafter, and soon after, Carter and his English lord friend who accompanied him on the expedition both died, one of a mysterious illness, the other by a spider bite. Within five years, all who had been on the expedition, as well as the local workers, were dead. There was a curse placed on anyone who opened the tomb, and a lot of black magic was invested in keeping it closed. Carter and his group disturbed this and suffered the fate of absorbing the negative energy invested in the objects in the tomb. That energy still held its effect."

Michael then related how many collectors who found old artifacts, such as swords and knives with a negative charge, might suffer as a result, such as one local collector he knew.

"He sells many blades used in wars and is often ill, because he continues to draw in the negative energy from all those battles."

After lunch, we headed to the fossil room. There were standing skeletons of huge dinosaurs with long tails, ancient monster-like birds, and leaping cats that once roamed the earth.

We tried more sensing and feeling, and I concentrated on depending on the psychic senses rather than logic. To help me,

Michael fired a series of questions at me to which I was to respond immediately and intuitively.

"What color are you sensing now?... What's the environment like?... What kind of food do you see the animal eating?

"Just experience and feel," Michael reminded me. "Though you may be influenced somewhat by what you know and your imagination filling in some details, you can assess what you are picking up psychically through the anomalous details—things you don't know that aren't common knowledge. Then, later, when you discover those things are true, that will help to validate your psychic perceptions."

We continued on, trading comments about what we were picking up.

Then, we came to a large specimen with heavy squat leg bones and splayed foot bones that looked like hooves.

"Now try this," Michael suggested, "without looking at the write-up."

Again I went into a kind of trance-like meditation in which I gazed ahead without really looking. "I get a tank-like feeling," I said. "Maybe a hippo. I get a sense of water, perhaps a river. This is a very slow moving, heavy, lumbering animal."

When I finished, Michael pointed to the description which read: "The North American Rhinoceros. One group were hippo-like forms most commonly found on rocks, interpreted as old stream channels, further supporting the suggestion that they lived like the hippos of today."

"That would appear to be pretty right on, wouldn't you say?" Michael commented. "Good work; by trusting your intuition you can get some real information from these fossils. Fossils are much safer to work with than artifacts, since what was put into artifacts is an unknown factor. Now, we'll move onto the marine display. We will project some energy to stimulate the fish."

We went onto the next exhibit and stopped in front of a large tank with three fish in it, each about six inches long. One was a sand shark, Greta told me, a tan, fuzzy, tube-shaped fish with a bottle-like nose. Another, a flat whitish fish with large black stripes. The last, an ugly scaly fish with a fat body, bulging eyes, and a bumpy tail.

As we observed them, they were gathered at one end of the tank, just resting over the pebbles on the bottom of the aquarium.

"Now I'll stimulate the fish," Michael announced. He knelt down and gazed intently at the one with bulging eyes. He explained, "I'm trying to make him believe there's another fish behind him by visualizing that fish."

We watched silently for a few minutes, and then suddenly the scaly fish began to arch its back and flap its tail.

"There you see," proclaimed Michael. "It has started to move, and its eyes are swiveling back, because it thinks there could be something there, though it's not sure what."

Greta concentrated on the one with black stripes, and announced that she was trying to encourage it to come forward. After awhile, it moved out of the group and swam to the top of the tank.

On my turn, I focused on the sand shark and imagined energy projecting out from the center of my forehead and pushing the fish to change position. After a few minutes, he swiveled his eyes at me and then looked away. Michael encouraged me to continue trying to get the fish to go where I wanted it to go.

"Look, I'll demonstrate," he said.

He focused on the striped fish which was moving back and forth in the upper tank.

"I'll try to get him to come back and move into this position." He pointed to a nearby spot, then, intently, stared at the fish, from time to time calling to it like a cat. At first, the striped fish continued swimming back and forth, though as it neared Michael's end, it hovered for a few moments, before swimming back, and after a few minutes began to swim in circles in front of Michael's end of the tank.

"Now that I've got his attention, I'll try to position him."

As he focused alternately at the fish and the selected spot, the fish circled a little closer, then brushed the side of the tank before moving away.

"Well, that's close enough," said Michael, breaking his concentration. "Now you try again."

I changed my position to focus on the same fish with stripes, which was now swimming back and forth along the side.

"Come on. Work, work," I thought to myself, as I tried to will the fish to break its sweep in front of me and move to the left or right. I visualized my energy moving out, latching onto the fish, pulling it to me. Now and then, it seemed to break its long, sweeping swim and hover in front of me.

Michael coached me from the side. "Now, just a little more. Keep that visualization. Pull him over. Just think of it like catching a fish, then throwing it back. Keep the visualization positive, imagining that you want only to move him, and that you mean him no harm."

Finally, the fish was a few inches away from the spot which I had selected. It stopped, gazed at me as if we had created some special connection, and then it swam away. I broke my gaze, and stood up, feeling drained from the concentration.

"Very good," Michael commented. "I'd say you drew him to you. And I saw him poised there, as if you had him with your will. We'll go to see the gems now."

We went on to enter a room with rows and rows of cases containing hundreds of glittering and colored stones of just about every hue and tone.

"This time," Michael announced, "you want to feel the essence of each stone. Use your seeing exercises, breathe it in, feel it through your hands. You want to use all your senses, and notice how you get a different feeling from each one."

As we walked by several cases, Michael picked a stone here and there to concentrate on, and gave me a running commentary. "Okay, from that fluorite I get a dark, flat feeling...from the halite, a salt-like crystal, I get a strong tingling energy...from the rhodochosite, a reddish stone, I sense more vitality, I can feel it just leaping out at me...from that anglesite, which is orange, translucent, I get a light, tingly feel."

When I was asked to try, I reported my observations, being reassured not to try to compare sensations to be sure of the "right" answer. "I'm only interested in your feelings, what you sense. Any differences could be due to our different energies interacting with the stone," commented Michael. I relaxed and just tried to feel. Meanwhile, Michael seemed pleased with my report. "Very good. You can feel differences in stones, and can sense that some have much more power than others.

"For example, this one." We stopped in front of a large chunk of a translucent, whitish, crystal. "Now here's a good thing to do with a crystal," he suggested. "Draw the energy out of the air and through the crystal into you. Just feel it coming in a kind of L-shape, and then coursing through your body. The advantage of crystals is that they act as a filter, so that you can pull in pure energy, and feel yourself replenished that way."

We moved on, and this time, Michael pointed out some of the differences he noticed to help me feel. "See if you can notice these subtle differences," Michael said. For example, in front of an aqua-blue chunk of turquoise, Michael observed: "Notice how it feels soothing and peaceful. Its energy is nice and smooth. But, with the white topaz, we also feel a soothing energy, but in a heavier way." In front of a white opal that seemed to dance with light, he commented: "Now this one is very high energy. I can even feel it in my heart. It's like it's beating faster, as if the high energy has stimulated this."

I stood in front of the opal myself and tried to breathe in the energy for a few minutes. Soon I felt a wave of pulsating energy pass through me.

"A good way to get an energy charge isn't it?" said Michael, and we moved on to a large, round, crystal ball on a pedestal. The sign indicated it was one of the largest, completely perfect crystals in the world.

"We'll do something special with this," Michael said. "Just concentrate on projecting your energy into the ball, and try to get a cloud of energy to form inside. As the cloud forms, you'll notice flickers as you put your energy in, and then the energy you have injected will all cloud up." I nodded that I thought it looked a little foggy. "So now I'll try to project in some pure energy, and now, there...you'll see a bluish light for a second." I said I wasn't sure I saw it. "Well, it was very quick," Michael said. "In any case, this process of projecting energy at the ball is a good way to do a reading. As you look in, you'll see images form in the cloud as you ask your questions, and then you can interpret those to do your reading."

We concluded our visit to the gems and minerals with a visit to the vault. Here there were several cases of small, precious stones, including jades, emeralds, opals, and diamonds.

"Here we can feel a very strong and refined power," Michael observed. "There's a higher frequency of energy here, so you'll feel more of a charge."

Greta reported she sensed the higher frequency of the energy and felt her whole body tingling. I focused on my sensations, and did feel more energized than before.

"Good," Michael responded. "We're at a real vortex of concentrated energy here. When you are sensitive, you can pick that up. It's like your whole body is vibrating at a faster rate, because you are picking up the energy from the stones. But then, notice the subtle differences in the individual stones."

Michael asked me to stand in front of a few stones and breathe in their energy through my hands and nose. "This rose crystal," he pointed out, "is more energetic. You can really feel it putting the energy out, and so it's especially useful for energizing. But this smoky crystal tends to pull the energy in. That's why these kind of crystals are often used as protective stones to attract negative energy. Then they pull it away from the wearer."

As we walked on, I wondered, "Is there any real physical effect on the body from all these stones?"

"You bet there is," Michael responded. He led us over to the emeralds to demonstrate. "For example, look at these emeralds. They feel expanding, but restful, and you'll find you not only feel more relaxed yourself with these, but your body will slow down, too. On the other hand..." He led us over to a case where a large, oval-shaped opal shimmered and glittered in the center. A circle of smaller opals in different colors and sizes ringed it, and they seemed to sparkle with energy, too. "...If you look at these opals, you'll feel they speed up your energy. They're alive, and can increase the vibrations of the body, which you can sense since your body is moving faster as well.

"These objects are really affecting your body. It is not your imagination, and your psychic abilities can pick it all up. They receive cues from your sensations, your feelings, and from the actions of your body. It's important to pay attention, however, because it's in the real use of psychic ability that the gemstones become powerful; otherwise they remain inert rock. When you have the ability to draw energy from them or manipulate it through them, you can sense their vibrations and tune into their individual uniqueness and essence. And you can use these objects for other purposes, such as to pick up information or for healing. But without this developed ability, the average person will just see a colorful or pretty rock. Then, too, while there may be real energy in these stones—or in anything used as a power object—what is most important is the energy that comes from the user; because the user must be able to see, focus, and direct his or her own energy properly through the object in order to pick up the information these objects contain or use them for power in any way.

Then, after we had a chance to similarly breathe in and feel some of the most precious gems in the collection—the diamonds and rubies—we were on our way back. As we drove along, I asked Michael whether he used his sensing and breathing all the time naturally.

"We are all constantly breathing in and tasting things, but at times one may not want to experience and feel so much. So becoming more sensitive can become a problem at times, especially in an intense or overpowering situation or if you feel very tired and don't want all that input. Thus, it is important to also learn to shut down. For example, if you sense a great influx of negative energy, or just a high level of input that becomes very distracting, it's good to learn to shut off the impressions coming in as a means of control. One way to shut down is through meditation, which helps to ground you. When you work as a shaman, you may receive an overload of sensations, including psychic ones. If you can bring this energy back inside yourself, and then bring in your antenna as well, you will feel much better. Your energy will still be high, but you'll feel more relaxed, more balanced, and much more at peace.

"The process works a little like using ear plugs to avoid the extra noise. And this is where the black color in the chakra mediation can help you, because black is a very restful, grounding color. When you visualize it while you meditate, you will become calm.

"Or, perhaps you might want to use protective clothing to shield and ground you. Something solid can serve as a barrier between you and outside impressions. For example, I know a

Tarot reader who wears gloves when she works. They are effective in cutting off potential sensations."

"Can't you just stop all the sensations mentally?" I asked.

"No, not after you have passed a certain point and have learned to open up. Once you have become involved in this kind of psychic mastery, you will stay involved, even if you are not paying attention. You are always sensitive and aware to some degree. But then, you can and should pull back at times, especially when the sensations are particularly intense. Paying attention to warning signals prevents the intake of negative energy, or provides the information necessary for appropriate response action to any danger, such as we felt in the museum in front of the stela. Realize also that everyday life can wear you down. For instance, you need to be especially aware of energy vampires. These people have a type of personality that draws your energy away, leaving you low and more open to disease."

"What kind of people?" I asked.

"Well, people who are especially critical, judgmental, angry, hostile, or negative, are examples. Or anyone who tends to take you over is, too. If you feel exhausted when you are talking to someone, take this as a sign that your energy is being sapped. Then, too, there may be places that are draining, such as being out in an angry and frustrated crowd during the Christmas shopping rush.

"Be ready during these times to shut down or to leave the situation, so you aren't overwhelmed. Alternatively, you may need to call up additional energy to replace any you lose. The idea is to remain balanced.

"Remember that we pay a price for the extra sensitivity we enjoy from life, in that we must remain alert to protecting ourselves against the negative energy in life as well."

Then we were back at the hotel. Michael dropped me off, reminding me to continue the practice of my breathing and color chakra exercises. I went upstairs to take a nap, feeling the need to rest after expending all that energy. In a few hours I would be back at Michael's to move on to the next lesson, one I really needed now—working with energy for improved health.

# CHAPTER EIGHT

## *LEARNING ABOUT HEALING THE SHAMAN WAY*

A few hours later, with my energy restored by the nap, I returned to Michael's. Greta was already there and Paul had joined us. Michael announced that Paul would conduct tonight's class, indicating that Paul was the expert in healing in the group.

Paul began by explaining why health is so important for someone involved in shamanism. "You need good health if you are going to be effective as a shaman," Paul asserted. "You've been learning a great deal on the raising and use of energy, and have discovered the importance of self-defense. All of these processes employ tremendous amounts of energy, and you need the ability to maintain your energy at a level sufficient to accomplish these things. If balance isn't maintained, illness can result. Then, too, you want optimum health in order to operate at the peak of your powers, and to assist in healing more quickly if any injury or disease occurs."

Paul turned to an illustration on the blackboard which featured an upside-down triangle, with the words: *spirit, mind,* and *body* written along the sides.

"You want to think of health as a state of the harmonious unity of the body, mind, and spirit. Your health affects your whole being. As the Orientals have long believed, all aspects of the being are one and the same; they are part of a total unity, and if one is out of balance, the rest will soon follow.

"Healthy practices are vital for the shaman. He or she must practice the proper energy gathering techniques. Also essential are the proper diet, exercise, and breathing techniques. The physical body is also an energy being, composed of energy and emanating energy as it acts. In turn, it consumes or inputs energy to sustain or renew itself."

Greta wanted to know what kinds of energy sources the body uses.

"These sources can be just about anything," Paul responded. "For example, you can gather energy from the vibrations of the stones around you, from the sun, the moon, and from colors. Anything can act as a source, but what can limit or block us in the ability to reach out and draw on this energy is our own make-up. Each person has his own signature and his own means of using this energy.

"That's important for understanding what an individual needs or what's wrong with the person. They teach in Oriental medicine that each individual can display different symptoms for the same disease. So it becomes important to learn the special combination needed for each person, including yourself. One way to obtain this knowledge is through psychometry. In the process of your meditation, you can psychometrize yourself to see the state of your body, or do the same to someone else.

"Start at the feet, and read each part until you come to the top of the body. As you read, you may find unexpected blocks or holes in the energy field, which could be old injuries, stress, or the beginnings of disease. Once you sense the source of the problem, work on eliminating it through will power or through simple healing techniques."

"How do you find out what's wrong?" I asked.

"Well, you need to get a picture of how you feel, and your own body energy is the best guide to that. Essentially, your body responds in the form of feelings, and then your intuition acts to interpret those feelings. For example, if you are around someone who wishes you harm, you may experience a sensation of an energy drain. Then you need your intuition to interpret what is happening, and this interpretation is a physical act. Therefore, gaining this understanding is a threefold process. It starts with your feelings, draws on your intuition, and then you interpret and verbalize what you feel. As you become more sensitive, the verbal advice from your intuition will increase."

"How can we work on increasing our sensitivity," asked Greta, "and thus make the intuition more available?"

"A number of ways," answered Paul. "For one, you can diagnose yourself through your breathing. Psychometrize yourself as you energize yourself through your breath. Second, get some regular exercise. You might want to take up the martial arts or some form of yoga. Use any method of exercise to promote good health, unblock your energies, and maintain good energy flow. You will increase your energy level and find yourself more resistant to disease.

"Third, watch your diet and avoid things that are unhealthy such as heavy doses of chemicals or red meat. Cut down or eliminate entirely any alcohol or smoking. These habits can constrict the blood vessels and add chemicals to the body. When you open the blood vessels up by avoiding such items, you open up the psychic channels, since everything is linked."

Paul also recommended avoiding any addictive substances, even coffee. "You want to keep the body as healthy and free as possible."

He then addressed the importance of using techniques to stay calm and relaxed. "It helps if you can give yourself occasional rest stops, or use methods to calm yourself in difficult situations. These methods can include meditation, silence, patience, or just reminding yourself of your purpose. Use one of these techniques wherever you feel yourself tensing up, to keep your energy from getting scattered or spent unnecessarily. So many people expend their energy in anger or for no purpose, and then find themselves tired or ill for no reason. If you can exercise control, you can keep this from happening to you.

"However, I realize that some situations in life can present a lot of pressure. For example, if you find yourself the victim of someone's screaming or anger, pull back and take a deep breath, and then marshal your forces so you effectively handle the problem with the minimum amount of stress. It helps to create a sense of detachment, because getting involved is what results in stress build-up. This detachment takes practice. You might try seeing yourself watching the situation from outside your body."

Paul continued his list of suggestions on increasing sensitivity and intuition. "You should also continue to practice your regular seeing, pineal gland stimulation, breathing, or other sensitivity exercises. These are important, and as you increase in sensitivity, you can learn to draw on good energy from the environment, or avoid any negative energy, either by changing the situation or by leaving."

Then Paul had some suggestions for working with these sensitivity exercises. "It helps to take one sense at a time and work on developing that. You can work on listening, the sense of smell, on sight, and on feeling. Whatever sense you are using," he urged, "call on that sense to get an impression of where you live, where you work, the whole world around you. In turn, this will help to make you more sensitive in all areas and better able to perceive how your environment is affecting you.

"This can be especially important in sensing negative energies, which you will find can happen in three ways," Paul continued. "First, you could feel your energy being drained. Second, you could be expending too much of your energy, and finally, someone could be directing negative energy at you personally. Whatever the circumstance, you can counter with calming or reflective techniques. In situations where the energy is being directed at you, you can respond by bouncing it back at the one who projected it."

Paul pointed to the triangle once more. "Now," he announced, "there are three key things that each of the three aspects of the whole being need for proper health." Next to the word *mind* on the triangle, he wrote the words: "challenges," "emotion," and "relaxation;" next to *spirit*, the words: "magic," "meditation," and "confidence;" and next to *body*, he wrote: "food," "herbs," and "exercise." "This is what the ideal human body should strive for," he said. "Now let me explain.

"First, for the proper health of the mind, you need mental challenges. Things like games, balancing your check book, working at a job you love, things that keep you mentally stimulated and alive. Secondly, the mind needs you to have a good emotional make-up. If it is out of balance, you must do what you can to correct things, since positive emotions flow through like high-energy nourishment, while negative emotions act like poisons to pollute the mind. Lastly, your mind needs relaxation, to counter any stress or fatigue. You might try music, fantasy, or other mental relaxation."

Then Paul briefly turned to the needs of the body, mentioning many of the cautions I had heard before from other people involved in nutrition and healing. Thus, he recommended things like plenty of fresh fruits and vegetables, and warned against the potential pollution of red meat. "At one time," he observed, "shamans could consume red meat as a power food, but today, there are so many hormones and other chemicals injected into the meat that unless you are sure the meat is perfectly natural, it would be best to stay away from it."

Paula also mentioned herbs and teas as good for relaxation. In fact, he suggested, "Herbalogy is a good field of knowledge for a shaman, since it can be of value in healing matters." He went on to suggest various forms of exercise—such as running, breathing, walking, and jogging as a way of "getting the blood moving. You want to participate in these types of activities, because the mind can become sedentary if the blood doesn't move fast enough."

But most of all, Paul wanted to emphasize the needs of the spirit, because, he explained, "This is usually the most neglected area of all. People take it for granted or don't acknowledge the needs of spirit at all. This is unfortunate, as the unsatisfied spirit can pull the mind and body down with it. For the shaman, this awareness of spirit is particularly important, because we work on the level of spirit and use this knowledge to aid the body and mind."

He pointed to the chart. "Now first, the spirit needs magic or some sense of religion. This is food for the soul. Secondly, you need to employ meditation to increase your spiritual awareness and strength. Finally, the spirit needs confidence, which acts as the wellspring or source of your power. It's like your inner gyroscope which lends you your sense of assurance that you are going in the right direction, that you are always on course. This doesn't mean you need to be absolutely perfect; you may make mistakes. But with an inner confidence, you can know that things will eventually turn out right, and that you have the ability to change things for the better. This sense in turn keeps you healthy, because you believe in yourself and in what you do. You won't let the occasional slings and arrows of fate pull you down, because you are still in charge; things will work out and get better, because you are in control.

"Or perhaps think of it this way," Paul offered. "If you feel confident, you won't let your occasional defeats pull you down. Rather, you will use your successes to nourish you, and you will cherish your successes even if they are small. In turn, these successes will contribute to this confidence, because if you treasure it, just one success can overcome many defeats. So honor your successes, and this will contribute to the confidence your spirit needs.

"Another important point," he went on, "is to realize that there are many paths to that success and to a totally whole and unified being. You can emphasize one of these aspects of the whole being far more than the others; but then your success in that area will stimulate the other areas to develop even more to come into balance.

"For instance, the extraordinary athlete, who has gained his success by honing his body to the extremes of perfection, has let the body predominate. But this development in turn stimulates the mind and spirit as well; for example, the excellent runner runs at his best when the mind and spirit are guiding him along.

"Those who pursue the highest development of the mind, such as our foremost thinkers, likewise need to have their bodies functioning effectively and their spirit in a calm and relaxed place, so they are free to pursue their mental endeavors without experiencing conflicts and blocks that might hold them back.

"The same goes for the shaman or magician who has chosen to emphasize the path of the spirit. It's not possible to work at the height of your powers unless your mind and body are in harmony also. And as you develop your spiritual gifts, you can use your abilities to overcome any problems of the mind and body. All aspects of the being want to remain in harmony. If you chose the path of the shaman, know that each person is different and has his own particular calling. I've chosen the path of the healer, and in my healing I use mental counseling as well as body techniques, whereas other healers might work with herbs and natural objects. There are many different paths, and all can lead to the truth. Choose the one that is right for you, and use your sensitivity and intuition to find your own way.

"For everything is interconnected—mind, body, spirit, and your intuition and awareness, which you can use in helping you develop in each of these areas. And balance is what holds all this together. You want to find the average mean or moderation in all things, such as a reasonable state of balance or compromise between attention and neglect. For example, too much love can be suffocating, too little can result in isolation and alienation; so either can bring harm to the whole person. By the same token, if someone doesn't like to be touched or to touch, this may be a sign of imbalance. On the other hand, people consider someone who touches too much to be strange. This is an imbalance in the opposite direction. The goal is thus to find a center point. Having found this center, you will feel complete and whole.

"So that's why," Paul concluded, "we stress the importance of a balanced training program if you want to develop your abilities as a shaman, as well as enjoy the good health you need to do this. And that's why the three aspects of being are so important. You need them all. Physical training, art, games of strategy, the martial arts, work on the psychic centers and the emotions—all of these can be a part of a shamanic training program, because these all cause stimulation and growth to take place in the different parts of your being. You need to develop them all, and I can't stress that enough."

And with that the first part of the class ended, and we went into the kitchen to take a break. As we got up, Paul told us, "After our break, we'll talk about using your energy points and raising energy. Then I'll show you some energy exercises you can use to stimulate all parts of your being, become more alert, use your energy more efficiently, and promote better health."

# CHAPTER NINE

## *WORKING WITH ENERGY*

After our break, Paul announced, "Now, let's talk about some techniques for working with energy," and we returned to the living room.

"First, we'll talk about the energy points," Paul said. He pointed to an outline of a human form on a board marked with dozens of circles all over the body. "There are three main types of energy sites or channels through the body where the flow can exit or enter.

"Ports or energy vents are where the energy flows out. They're like portholes in the aura, since they bring in energy as well. If there is a blockage somewhere, the excess energy can get stuck at these points, and you will sense an abundance of energy, and also find it hard to project energy into the environment.

"Secondly, there are energy intake areas, which are also sensory centers, such as the palms of the hands and the soles of the feet.

"And finally, there are the major areas which most people are familiar with and which correspond to the chakra system. These centers are sensory to some extent, but in general, they gather and channel energy through the system. Thus they are more like storehouses or amplifiers of the psychic circuit system, and they help conserve energy. These sites correspond to the acupuncture meridians, and they function to create lines of force which supply the body with energy. So these centers are all interlinked as one large energy network, and this network needs to keep its centers free and the flow of energy moving, so the energy can circulate and the body breathe freely. Then, too, some of these sites are powerful sensory centers that can pick up things from the environment as well as being healing centers. What we teach here is based on twelve years of working with energy directly in the field, so you won't find all of this in books on the traditional systems."

Paul now proceeded to describe the various sites.

"There's a spot at the base of the neck which is very sensitive, although it's not generally identified in other systems. However, if you direct energy at this site, you can calm the individual down and help him feel more peaceful. However, directing negative energy at this site will cause depression."

Paul pointed to another area at the base of the skull. "Now this center is connected with consciousness, among other things. Some energy directed here can return an unconscious person to a conscious level. The energy placed at this spot can work on the individual's metabolic level and increase his respiratory rate."

Next, he indicated an area along the spine between the shoulders. "Here," he pointed out, "a great deal of energy accumulates, and it can be employed to help revitalize someone. For example, I was with someone once who had collapsed after expending a tremendous amount of energy in a psychic exercise. I reached out and directed some of my own energy into him at this point, and then I used some light slapping to spread the mingling of our energies through this area. In a few minutes, he was completely revived.

"This area," Paul pointed to the top of the head, "is used mainly to take energy in, although it is sensory in nature as well, and can be used to induce a trance by depressing the energy at this site. You can also induce a trance by applying a shutting down process to the chakra centers. This is what happens when a person goes into a meditative state and leaves his body. To bring him back, stimulate the centers."

Paul went on to discuss some less commonly known centers. "Take the back of the arms," he observed. "They're not generally considered to be either an energy center or an acupuncture spot, but they are a key area used by shamans, because there is a great deal of sensitivity here, and it's both a venting site and a sensory one. It is common to use this site to psychometrize one's surroundings.

"Then too," he lifted his foot, "the Achilles tendon can be used to intake energy from the surroundings or to draw energy out of someone which will calm them. Directing energy at this point will wake them up. Also note that in all of these healing techniques I have discussed, it is not necessary for you to have direct vision of the particular body part, although this can make it easier. You can just visualize the area of the body where you want to direct energy."

Greta had a question. "How close do you have to be to use this visualization effectively?"

"It's best to have physical contact in the beginning, when you are first learning these techniques," Paul answered, "but as your ability develops, the distance apart can increase. In fact, you can even talk to people over the phone or do this without the person being present. Just visualize the person and his surroundings, and feel a connection over the astral waves."

Paul turned back to the chart. "A few other important sites in shamanism are the palms of the hands, the bottoms of the feet, the backs of the arms, the solar plexus, the third eye, and the crown chakra. All of these can be used to breathe in the energy around you. When you are not using these centers, however, be sure to close them down, so they're not vulnerable to intaking negative energy."

Paul now gave a sign to Michael to dim the lights.

"We'll do some sensitivity and energy work now," Paul said. "We'll use the chakra centers to induce a brief trance for relaxation, but then they will come back on, so you are very sensitized. It's a quick and effective way to bring about a heightened but relaxed state of sensitivity, which is especially helpful for psychic healing."

"What's the best state to be in for healing or being healed?" Greta wanted to know.

"Well, if you are going to be healed, you want to do a trance meditation to shut down your energy points or centers," Paul observed. "You want to depress these centers to prepare yourself to be more receptive to the healing energy. On the other hand, if you are going to project some healing energy, you want to do a trance initially to relax, so you are in a more receptive state. But then, you need to raise your energy level with, for example, a chakra meditation, so your energy is available for healing."

"I'll lead the energy relaxation technique now," said Michael, and he asked us to get into a comfortable, relaxed position. "I'll be using the light switch technique," he said. "It's one of the most effective ways to either visually stimulate or depress the energy centers."

Greta and I got into a relaxed position, with our feet planted firmly on the floor and our hands outstretched. At first Michael's voice sounded firm and clear, and then gradually it came from further away, as I felt my body shutting down, while my mind remained receptive and alert.

"Just start by taking a deep breath," Michael began. "Let it out slowly and relax. Allow your body to relax... Let your body go limp... Now, on your second breath, relax even more... And finally, with your third breath, you feel even more relaxed... Now I'd like you to just float there for a minute. Feel your body, feel yourself..."

Then, as we both drifted off into this spacey, relaxed state, Michael began the exercise to depress our energy centers by shutting off the light switch at each site.

"Now first I'd like you to visualize a light switch on your left foot," I heard Michael say. "Then visualize yourself reaching down and switching this to the off position. As you do so, feel your left foot completely relax. Feel the energy go to a state of complete restfulness. And if you don't feel this at any time, go back to this site and shut it off."

Then, Michael continued the process, indicating one site after another. "Next picture a light switch on your right foot and shut this center off... Now go to the back of your left calf... Picture the switch on your right calf... Now to your left and right hips... Now you are switching off the area slightly above the genital region and below your belly button... Now go to your belly button. Feel the relaxation spread to your stomach and lower abdomen... Now to the center of your chest. Switch it off and feel the relaxation radiate out to the muscles of your chest and your rib cage... Next experience the relaxation at the level of your right and left collar bone... Next switch off the switch at the base of your spine...Now onto the shoulder blades and feel the muscles of the shoulders relax... Next visualize a switch on your right and left hands and shut it off... Now experience that switch going off on your forearms... Now go to the base of your throat near the collar bone... Now shut off the area of your third eye and relax your face and your forehead... And lastly, at the top of your head, shut it off and completely relax."

Then, after we floated for a few minutes in this totally relaxed and shut-off state, Michael began the healing part of the exercise. He spoke softly and gently, his voice like a faraway drone.

"Okay, now as you breathe, visualize your energy coming into you as you breathe in, and circulate it into your chest. From there, visualize it dispersing throughout your body, radiating energy from your chest to your abdomen and legs, and finally into your feet. Then, the energy radiates out into your arms and forearms, to your fingers, up along your spine, and through your throat into your head. Feel the energy circulate throughout, and pay special attention to any area where it does not seem to flow smoothly."

As we floated there doing this, Michael and Paul, who had both raised their own energy with a quick chakra meditation, visualized themselves sending healing energy to any areas where we experienced blockages. I noticed a feeling of infused energy even while I remained relaxed.

Then Michael said, "Now we are going to start to come back. Reach out with some of this energy, and visualize a light switch in the area of your left foot and turn it on, feeling energy and consciousness return to the site. Feel the switch on your right foot, and feel the stimulation and energy as you breathe return to your body." He went through all the previous sites mentioned before, ending at the crown chakra. "And now, feel the sense of vitality radiating throughout you, and slowly bring yourself to a normal waking state. Open your eyes slowly, and feel the energy return as you return to the room."

When we were back, Michael suggested that this was a good technique to use for both self-hypnosis and self-healing.

"It's a good way to turn yourself on and off, circulate energy with your breath, and to look for energy blocks when doing this. Then, should you experience any blocks, you can breathe in energy to the areas that need healing or more energy. Of course, if anything is seriously wrong, you will be aware of it, and can go for professional help.

"Also, it's very important to come back gradually by turning on each of the centers separately. You can do this quite rapidly when you are used to it, but you always need to touch all of the centers, so that you don't experience any blocks in your energy flow."

"In any event," Paul added, "one reason this kind of technique works so well, is because it focuses the mind, so that in this heightened state of awareness, the mind is highly receptive."

Paul then had some energy channeling and crystal healing techniques to show us, but first he wanted to point out why it was so necessary for us to use them.

"You see," he said, "when you enter into the magical world of the shaman, particularly when you go out on your own, you are subjecting yourself to spiritual hazards as well as spiritual glories. You can easily find your energy sapped, and thus it is important for you to learn the feel of your own energy and how to correct any problems, so that you can operate at full capacity."

Michael pulled out some small crystals and placed them on the table. He continued the discussion. "Besides energy channeling for yourself and others, you can also employ tools to assist with your work. These can be both natural and created ones. One type of natural approach is herbalogy, but we won't go into that here. Another powerful tool is the use of crystals. Essentially, a plain crystal functions as an amplifier of your energy, so it's excellent for the manipulation of power."

Michael held up a crystal that was about four inches long, and gazed at it intently. "Now you will see a beam of energy issuing out of it as I do my work," he announced. "And it is even easier to see this against a dark background." He flicked off the lights and held the crystal in a dark, curtained area of the room.

"Yes, I can see what you mean," Greta commented. "It seems like a fuzzy, white light projecting a few inches from the end of the crystal."

I nodded to indicate that I also saw a whitish fuzzy glow.

Then, putting down the crystal, Michael briefly held his hand over one of the small, votive candles that was burning on the table. "What I'm doing now," he explained, "is raising my energy. I was feeling low on energy, so I am holding my palm towards the candle, and I'm visualizing the energy from the light drawn up into my body. Then it radiates through me. It's a good way to get a quick charge of energy."

He picked up the crystal. "Another way to increase your energy is to visualize the energy being drawn up from the light source through a simple crystal, into your palm, and then through your body. The crystal will amplify the original energy from any source. As you draw this energy through the crystal, direct it from your hand through your arms to your solar plexus, which is the seat of your hara or will. As you sense the energy there, hold it. You can use your hands to help you hold them there by grasping your hands in front of the solar plexus in a cupping, pushing motion. Hold them there for a few moments, until the energy has fully radiated through your body."

"Do you need to use your hands to do this?" I wondered.

"In the beginning, it's probably a good idea, since they will help you experience that holding feeling. But as you become more adept, you can absorb and hold that energy at will without using any gestures, and you will do it more quickly also. Ultimately, your goal should be to do these energy raising and holding exercises from any position, even while moving. Initially, start with both hands, then go to one, and finally use no hands at all."

Next Michael handed Greta and me each a crystal. "Now, I have some exercises to show you in working with energy. First, hold the palm of one hand over the candle and breathe in its energy. As it circulates into your hara or the center of your will, feel the vitality charging you up."

We did this for several minutes and indicated that we felt more energized.

"Okay, now take the crystal and hold it near the flame. Breathe the fire's energy through the crystal this time into your solar plexus and then to your hara, and when you have breathed in a sufficient amount, move into your holding position and compare the feeling to the previous work."

Greta reported feeling more energized. I felt as if my concentration was more focused.

"And now, I want to show you how you can use that energy you have built up inside yourself," Michael indicated. He asked each of us to hold a crystal between our fingers and to project a little energy from the tip. "Then, move it over your hands with a brushing motion, and then over your arms. But don't touch the crystals," he cautioned. "You should notice a definite sensation."

"I feel a tingling sensation," Greta said.

"I feel like I'm drawing a line," I added.

"Good," said Michael. "That's the energy you're feeling. The tingling sensation is perfectly natural.

"Now I want you to hold out your hands," he continued. As we stretched them out, he picked up his own crystal and held it poised in the air over our hands. "I want to show you a crystal breathing technique. It's a little like acupuncture. I will breathe out as you breathe in while I point the crystal at your palm. Pull the energy up through your arm. Go ahead, and concentrate on your breathing."

We did this several times and Michael asked us what we felt.

"I felt my palm grow warmer," I commented.

"I felt as if a beam of light was going through my arm, and then it was filling my head with light."

"Good," observed Michael. "What we've done is an example of a direct energy transfer. It's very quick, and the energy went from me to each of you. The crystal amplified the work. This energy transfer can be used in healing or to psychometrize someone."

Then Michael asked Greta and me to face each other, so he could teach us mutual energy transfer techniques. "Each of you will send, then receive, then send back, so that you get a sense of energy going back and forth. I'll be showing you three different techniques, and I want you to notice the differences. You can use this for energy raising and for healing."

Greta and I positioned ourselves on the couch as Michael requested.

"I want you to start by holding hands," Michael instructed, "and run the energy out of your hands. Use your right hand to send and the left to receive." We started to do this. I visualized a cone of energy pouring out of my right palm, while I cupped my left palm, ready to receive. "Now be sure to send right away," he added, "otherwise, you can become very lightheaded, with all that extra energy coming in." After a few minutes, he asked us to let go. "But gently," he warned. "Just release gently. You don't want to snap back."

We spoke about the experience. Greta and I briefly mentioned the feeling of tingling in our hands, but Michael wanted us to pay even closer attention to some of the subtleties of this energy exchange we might have missed.

"Perhaps you may have noticed," he said, "the moment when you felt not only your own energy, but that of your partner as well. What you want to do is notice the qualitative difference between the two, since this can assist you in tuning into the essence. Then, you may have observed a point where the energies mingled, and here you want to re-experience the feeling of these energies linking. This knowledge is very important in healing, because when you can connect with the other person, you can send in your own healing energy on their energy level or wave length if you wish. That will provide a more effective result. Now position yourselves for the next exercise."

As we stood waiting, Michael continued.

"This time hold your hands above each other, about six inches apart, and just at the point where the edges of your auras touch. You want to have a slight link of connection. Now repeat the sending and receiving, and when you are done, gently pull away. Then ground out, to let your energy find it's center."

When we were done, Greta observed, "There seemed to be a connection with my breathing as we did this. When I was sending energy out, I was breathing out. When I received energy, I was breathing in."

"This is perfectly natural," Michael explained. "In fact, if your breathing is linked to the energy movement, it will help reinforce the process."

Then, Michael asked Greta and me to stand up, about four feet apart. "For this one," he said, "you want to get a little distance from your partner. What we'll be doing is a palm to palm transfer of energy. You will be sending, receiving, and sending the energy back again, but doing it at the same time to form a loop." We did this for about a minute, and I felt like the energy was swirling around in a continuous circuit. It reminded me of watching the edges of a spinning record on a turntable.

"And now gently separate," Michael instructed, and Greta and I slowly separated. "Then, take the grounded position to bring your energy back into your solar plexus." As before, we clasped our hands across our solar plexus.

Michael wanted to know how the last three exercises had felt, and what were their differences. We agreed that the last one had been the most powerful, even though we were more separated. I felt that the last one was like a blending of the energies into a continuous cycle.

"And I saw a beam of light as we did it," Greta added. "It was as if we were a rubber band connected. I sensed a complete circle, and felt as if there was a rope connecting our hands and running through us."

"Very good," Michael continued. "Now you see that physical contact is not necessary for the connection. Your energies link you, and this link can be used to sense and heal the other person."

Next, Paul had a special energy raising exercise for us. Greta and I sat on the couch, and Paul sat across from us in a comfortable chair, with his arms resting on the arms of the chair, his feet planted solidly on the floor. The room was lit only by candlelight.

He began with an explanation. "What I'll be doing is an exercise using the chakras. This will test your ability to perceive as I move the energy to the different levels of the chakras. I'll start by centering the energy in my hara or will center, which has a gathered umbrella shape, since I've been working with energy for some time. Instead of the concentrated energy ball, my energy has extended upward into the umbrella shape we talked about previously. I will gather this energy and send up fibers to create a bar of energy that moves straight up and back down again along the chakras, to create an energy loop within myself. As this energy moves up, I will see the color of its aura, and I will send it out as healing energy from one hand to the other, so you should be able to see the actual energy coming through. Perceive this energy, and notice what you feel about its functions and uses.

"The purpose of this technique is to open up the channels so that the healing energy comes through. It's a little like using two electrodes to stimulate impulses in an electronic device. In this case, I'm sending and transmitting psychic electric impulses within myself only. Essentially, I'm working with the inner "chi" energy which the Japanese talk about. It issues from the core and radiates out as a very powerful source of energy. This particular exercise is designed for you to be able to see this happening."

For the next few minutes Paul focused on his task, while we watched intently. He appeared like a faintly luminescent shape against the inky blackness, and I could barely see his hands moving as he brought them in and out and sometimes up and down to circulate the energy between them. As I watched, I saw a small, whitish, fuzzy projection extend up, and then it seemed to turn into a yellowish beam with a bit of purple above it. As he put his hands together, I noticed streaks and sparkles of energy between them, like a bouquet of flowers, and then this burst and dispersed like fireworks. Soon after, the energy calmed down and all was darkness again.

Michael asked us to report what we saw. Greta began.

"I first saw the energy bar come up through you," she said, "and it seemed you were stretching it, and growing taller as you sat. Your hands grew smaller, while you kept growing. I saw the glow of your aura rise up with this white energy beam inside it. A bar mushroomed out and came down, as you appeared to widen. You almost disappeared, then came back, and then you were even taller."

"Yes, he was expanding and contracting," Michael observed.

"As you mushroomed out," Greta continued, "I noticed a whitish, blue beam come out of your arms. It seemed as if a luminous lump of energy was between your hands. Towards the end, this all calmed down, and you melted into it. I saw you let your hands go and ground yourself, and then the energy bar and luminescence disappeared."

I next described my own experience.

"Excellent," Paul exclaimed when I was done. "You both have seen very well. Basically, what each person can expect to see with this exercise is the aura, the luminous center or egg inside, and the fibers going out, and both of you have seen something like this, plus even more. It's very good in your early stage of development as a shaman to be able to see so much. Also, notice that what you each saw could be an indication of what you need individually, since we tend to take in the energy and see what we need at the time for healing. For example, Gini saw some flowers and sparks. Greta talked about a bar of energy and a luminous coming together between her hands. This reflects your needs for different types of healing energy. Furthermore, if you don't need anything at the time, you may not see anything.

"Also, it's important to learn to trust what you see, because your belief helps you see and experience this energy, although not seeing does not make the energy any less real. The energy exists whether you see it or believe in it or not, though your desire to see something, to get some healing from the energy, does help to create it and enable you to see and experience it. In any case, your natural ability will show you that something is there when someone works with energy and you are aware. But if you want something further from that energy, such as healing for a problem, you will see that energy more clearly, and your needs will dictate the specifics of what you see. Later you can seek to interpret these specifics in more detail through self-examination or through counseling between you and a shaman."

I asked Michael to describe what he saw, since I expected that a master shaman with greater abilities could see more than we had. He provided a very complete description.

"In my case, I tend to see a great deal of detail on the mechanics of the results and their emanations, and I pick up on what others are sending as well. So I generally see an overall or total picture."

He turned and addressed Paul directly.

"I saw various energies moving through your body and being brought up by your breath. As the process continued, I saw sparkles of luminescence at your base, moving up in flashes. When it reached its height, I saw blue sparks rising from the abdominal area to an area below your solar plexus, where a wall of energy made up of many colors and sparks shot up into your chest area. From here the energy seemed to expand.

"I felt it moving up the back of your neck, and it expanded through the front of your head and gathered near the third eye. It stayed very solid there and expanded some more. Meanwhile, there was a continuing activity of sparks through all this.

"Once the energy peaked there, your head began to vanish, and soon your shoulders and upper torso did also. Meanwhile, the exhalation of your breath became longer, even though the intake remained normal. It seemed at times as if you were exhaling for one or two minutes, which was really quite amazing. This shows a definite and very remarkable control of your breath."

Michael paused for a moment, and then went on. "You came back in a most interesting and unusual way. I could still see you, but the rays of the candlelight shone through you, so you were translucent. As you brought your hands together, I could see the energy expanding from one side of you to another, and it was a very dark purple energy, heavy and thick. Then it lit up and became transparent, with lots of sparkles and flashes.

"This energy expanded out, and I saw it unwind and expand into the room. As it did so, you became solid again. You were a black silhouette, and suddenly you were very much present. There was no question but that your energy was grounded in you, and you were fully here in the room. You brought yourself back in the darkness, and it was just you again."

"Was that what you actually did?" I asked Paul. He was only too happy to explain.

"Well, everyone certainly saw a little differently," he commented.

"I started off by doing the color chakra meditation you learned, and I felt the colors fill me up as the energy gathered. I drew this into my basic core, so this energy was in a very refined state. Meanwhile, there was a gathering of energy around me, and my own aura expanded because of the attraction and radiation of this static electricity in the air. These bits of energy gathered in the air because of the great energy and heat I was creating with my breath. With each breath, I worked my way up the chakras. When I reached the top, I started the long exhalations. This would be my seventh breath." he observed.

"On the eighth breath, the energy traveled in a circular fashion, down in front and around to the bottom chakra. From the back of my spine, the energy came up over the crown and down, looping around. At the end of the ninth breath, I extended my hands, and then I projected my energy to create this continuous flow between them on the tenth breath.

"Finally, I shut down the projection of energy, and relaxed in feeling that sense of being I had created within myself. I felt a great floating sensation and a sense of oneness which was very deep and internal. At this point, I was aware of your presences again. But I was still too charged up and high to come back immediately. I couldn't talk, or if I tried, I would probably talk very fast. So I focused on diffusing the energy. I was still in a somewhat heightened state of awareness, but now the energy was more diffused. As I finally came back into a more ordinary state of consciousness, I felt as if I had been away for a very long time."

"Now be sure to note how much control all that took," Michael commented. "A great deal of discipline and concentration. The average person can't just sit down and do that."

"How long did it take you to be able to do that?" I asked Paul.

"Well, you might say it's the product of nine years of training and meditating everyday. It can be an excellent form of self-centering and self-healing, but my ability to get into the proper state of mind in a quick and focused way is due to regular practice. How long it would take someone else depends on them and their training. However, you must be careful not to attempt this exercise too soon into the early training period because it takes a tremendous amount of concentrated energy. Attempting it before you are ready could result in a tear of your energy fibers, damage your psychic centers, or cause you great mental or psychic strain."

Before the day's lessons were over, Michael had two simple, self-healing exercises to talk about, which would complete this phase of the training.

"These are best for simple injuries or aches," Michael said. He held out his right hand, which he had recently sprained in a martial arts class. It was wrapped in an ace bandage. "My simple injury can be an example. You would first gently message the injured area, using a spiraling-out motion. Start from the part of the extremity which is closest to the body, which would be the wrist here. Work your way down and out, and continue out into space. You are moving the energy down and out of the injured area, gathering it out with your working hand, and casting the energy from the injured part into space. With each successive wave of the massage, you are casting more of the energy out of you.

"After you do this enough times, and the muscles feel relaxed, take the working hand, and without touching the injured part, contact the aura and gently brush it down. Just project energy out of your hand to do this, and brush the negative energy out and away. Then, circulate a lot of energy through this injured area by breathing in and out through this area. Check the aura around it, noting how it looks. If any areas do not look as alive or vital, they are not projecting as well, and you may not have milked enough negative energy from them. If so, go back and repeat the whole process, with a special emphasis on that particular area. You need to repeat the whole technique if you want to be thorough and get the most out of it. If you miss any sections, some negative energy will remain and these sections will stay blocked."

"What kind of energy or feeling are you looking for to know you have done it properly?" I queried.

"You're sensing a smooth flow of energy. It should have the usual sort of length, intensity, or vividness you are used to. If not, go back and work on that part again until you get that strong vitality and flow."

"What if you have a cut rather than an injury?" asked Greta.

"If that is the case, you can't do a lot of massage, but you can do the brushing motions. Then, after you physically treat the injury, come back and do the brushing to remove the unhealthy energies. Finally, circulate the new, healthful energies through the area as before."

Michael tapped the top of his head. "Now here's another version of this technique, which is good for headaches or deep aches that can't be reached readily. Just bring the energy of your body to the affected area and circulate that energy through it. As you do, breathe out the harmful, negative energy, and replace it with a smooth and healthy energy by relaxing and willing away the pain. Just relax with each breath, and visualize the pain going out into space, where it is dissipated and replaced by a feeling of restfulness and well being."

When Michael finished, he sat down beside Paul. They had covered all they wanted to about working with energy for healing.

Michael asked, "Do you have any questions?"

I thought for a moment. "Well, yes," I said. "I'm bothered by knowing whether I'm really perceiving something or whether it's just my imagination. How will I know?"

"You will develop your confidence," Michael reassured me. "It's not just your imagination, and as you get more feedback, that will help convince you of your psychic ability. In fact, you may see things that I don't. You may be in situations where you see something no one else does. Thus, if you see some energy when you are working with someone, even if they are not consciously trying to project it, you should say something. It may be that they are leaking out some energy or have some negative energy they are not aware of. Maybe you can help heal them by that simple act. For example, you might just use a pat on the back, or send someone a rush of good, healthy energy, and help them feel healed at the time."

And on that note, the lesson ended.

"Tomorrow we will talk about mirrors and gateways, so be sure to bring your mirror," Michael said. "Then on Friday, you should be ready to do your own gateway and go for your next grade if you can."

It was already Wednesday. I had been immersed in this intensive, daily training for almost one full week now, and I had just two more days to go to see if I could make the test.

"Now remember to practice your regular exercises," Michael reminded me as I left, and I said I would.

# CHAPTER TEN

## *LEARNING ABOUT GATEWAYS*

Thursday afternoon, after writing up another chapter on my book, I decided to go to the beach in Malibu, a small coastal town north of Los Angeles, to try out some of the energy techniques I had learned. I set off about three in the afternoon, and was expected back at Michael's at six, so I didn't have a lot of time to work.

Today, as I drove, I concentrated on breathing in the environment around me. As a result I found I felt more vital and alive, and was more aware of the colors and sounds of the world around me, rather than driving as I usually do in a kind of semi-conscious automatic pilot state until I arrive at my destination. Now, instead, I felt I wanted to let every sight and sound in, and, as I passed the small beach houses and occasional patches of beaches and harbors, I felt a charge of freedom as I imagined the more languid pace of people living in these areas, and I felt the energy of my body slowing down as I imagined this. Then I savored this relaxed slowness, and even when I encountered a traffic jam on the highway, I remembered my energy techniques and projected my consciousness far outside myself, exploring the beaches and hills around me as I drove. I finally arrived at the beach, drove onto a soft dirt promontory by the side of the road, got out, and scrambled down the rocky path to the beach.

I walked south, with the ocean to my right, and I noticed the houses on the left perched on pilings that curved along the beach into the distance. I passed some signs that warned to watch out for metal barriers and fittings buried in the sand, and then I began to run. I felt the slap of my feet against the wet sand, and I imagined myself breathing in the very energy of the sand, sea, sun, and air as I ran, just as Michael and Paul had told me to do.

It felt exhilarating, and for a few moments, I felt light like air, as if I were not only running with it, but actually being lifted up by it, while the sun charged me with its light, and the sea with its pounding energy. I was breathing in the four elements here, and becoming them.

Suddenly, I heard the loud, deep bark of a dog, and then saw a dark, short-haired animal that looked like a mix of airedale, pit bull, and spaniel bounding for me. At once, I stopped running and froze. I glanced around. The beach was completely deserted and, for a moment, I trembled with fear as the barking dog came closer, acting as if it were defending its territory and I was an intruder.

Then, I remembered what Michael had said about projecting energy, and I began to draw in the energy I had gathered from the elements around me into my center. As I did, the waves of fear subsided, and I imagined myself projecting the energy fibers from my center out at the dog to push him away. At the same time, I glared at him, and I projected the intention out at him: "Go away... Go away."

Within seconds, the dog suddenly slowed to a lope and then stopped about twenty feet from me. His barking turned into a whine and then a whimper, and he looked at me uncertainly, as if he didn't know what had suddenly hit him. For a moment I saw him waiver, as if he was caught by a sudden fear about me and what I might do. And then, dropping his head, he turned and loped off, and I relaxed, feeling relieved, and let my energy projection go. I walked on feeling reassured and more confident about myself after this brief encounter, and I felt a greater sense of energy and power, too.

It was time to go back. The sun was nearly setting as I returned. I passed the spot where I had seen the dog, and as I walked through, stiffly, guarded, I noticed that I felt a heavy, almost palpable negative energy as I walked on. So this was what Michael had meant when we talked about negative energy lingering in an area. After I left the area, the negative cloud lifted, and the beach now seemed radiant, the water sparkling once again. Was this because of a change in the energy, too?

After about ten minutes, I was at my car, and soon on my way back to Michael's for the next lesson. When I arrived, Greta was already there. I sat on the couch and set up my tape recorder and notebook as usual, and then I told Michael about my time on the beach.

"Well, very good," he said when I was done. "You might consider that experience one more example of how the energy is very real—the way you felt, the way you chased off the dog."

Then, with his small green slate blackboard beside him, he began the lecture. He pointed to an odd, double-cone shape on the board."Tonight we'll be talking about the physics of working with gateways and mirrors. They're related, since your ability to make a gateway is aided by your ability to work with mirrors, and vice versa. In a sense, each is an outgrowth of the other.

"Basically, both are a very valuable tool for the shaman since they are a means of extending the will through space and time to a distant location by artificial means. Through the use of a gateway or a mirror, a shaman can project his will through what you might call hyperspace, transcending the limits of physical time and space, and thus directly entering other planes of reality."

"That's pretty far-out," I commented.

"Yes, but just put your preconceptions aside," he asked. "It will take some explaining, but there are some underlying principles to help explain this. Now, a gateway can be defined as a rift or hole in the fabric of reality. It's a doorway, which can be artificial or natural, between one dimensional plane and another, or between points on a given plane of reality, such as our physical one."

I asked him to define natural and artificial, and the term different planes.

"The natural gateways are already existing in nature; the artificial ones you create yourself. By different planes, I am referring to the difference between our physical world and the world of spirits.

"Now, there are a number of types of natural gateways. The Bermuda Triangle is probably one of the most famous, associated with all sorts of strange sightings and disappearances. There are many stories connected with it, and some descriptions are very characteristic of a shaman's experience with a gateway.

"In one case, there was a Coast Guard cutter out on a routine patrol. According to their logs, they picked up a dense body on their radar, which looked like fog. They investigated, and found that dense fog formed in a straight line before them, which is unlike any normal fog with ragged edges. When they entered the fog, their compasses went wild, and their electrical system had problems. They found it hard to make any headway, as if they were stuck in a place of very dense energy acting against them. Finally, they retreated and survived. Their description sounds very much like entering a gateway and coming back."

Michael's next story was even stranger. "In this case, an experienced aviator disappeared while he was making a radio transmission from his plane to the airport. The controllers picked him up coming inbound to the airport in Miami, but he radioed that he was lost. When they asked him to specify his position, he said his compass was out, and when he reported his visual sightings, he claimed there were some islands below him that weren't on his chart. The airport radar indicated he was over a populated coastline, but he was only seeing uninhabited islands below him. Also, witnesses in the inhabited areas near the airport heard the plane overhead, but no one could see it, even though it was a clear day. Eventually, the tower lost contact. Presumably, he ran out of fuel and crashed into the sea. Perhaps, this is a case where he entered a natural gateway and slipped out of present time and space.

"I bring up these cases because they parallel the experience of many shamans, including ourselves and Don Juan, as reported by Castaneda. When a shaman enters a gateway and passes into another reality, he also commonly enters what seems to be a very dense fog. Then, he steps out into the world on the other side. Commonly, too, these reports of shamans reflect a bending of time and space, where time stretches out or shortens, while objects appear or disappear, which parallels the accounts of instruments acting strangely and islands mysteriously being sited. The creation of these natural gateways, however, is not fully understood. They may be due to fluctuations of the earth's magnetic energies in that particular area. These forces may move or interact in some way to produce the water or foggy substance often involved. Perhaps in the case of the Bermuda Triangle, the gateway is there because water is a powerful conductor of electro-magnetic energy.

"In any case, the important thing for you to understand is that our present physical reality does not exist on only one plane. This reality is layered like an onion, in which there are multiple planes of reality existing simultaneously. For example, you may be operating in the present physical plane at the same time that other energies or spirits are functioning right around you on another, higher plane which you normally can't see, though you can with *seeing*.

"Another important point about gateways is that we can actually see them, if we have the ability to see into these other planes. We can see them because they represent a break in the fabric of the vital energy composing these planes—a concept sometimes referred to as the ether, a term spiritualists in the thirties commonly used. We perceive this energy as sparkles or flashes of energy in the air, which is what you have been doing since you started this training and first learned to see.

"Besides the ability to see, there are also certain states in the energy of the environment that are more conducive than others to enhancing this ability to view and create gateways. A foggy night is especially good, because physically, these altered planes of existence become more visible in this light. Also, this foggy atmosphere helps to create a better psychological state for this seeing in the human mind—the consciousness is more receptive, less focused on physical reality, and at the same time, the will is more activated.

"When there is real fog, the qualities of the energies in the environment are different, possibly because of the water vapor, so there is more electromagnetic energy in the air. Also, the fog has a kind of enclosing, wrap-around effect that can be very psychologically liberating, supporting a shaman's desire to act freer and to exercise his will. Further, the individual consciousness is more attuned to seeing into alternate realities, providing a better vision to see and to create gateways.

However, working in this fog can also be very dangerous, since it's so much easier to open up these gateways then. But, once this hole in reality is opened, things can easily come out of this gateway from another reality, and there are times when things enter these holes in reality and can't get back. Still, a well trained shaman can overcome such a risk later to enter and return through these gateways successfully, but it requires great focus, concentration, and personal power. There are other dangers as well which you should be informed of, too, so you are ready when you try your own gateway.

"One of the major ones is the possibility of beings from another reality entering ours. The shaman must possess the ability to send them back or to control them. I can give you an example of this.

"This occurred when you were working on *The Shaman Warrior*, and we were encamped in San Francisco during the night of Harvey and Serge's solo." My memory of that time was hazy. "It was a very foggy night," he went on, "when I cut a gateway in the fog, and a birdlike being suddenly flew out. This was very real and had the appearance of no known flying bird. Rather, it was more bat-like, with a blunt head, leathery wings, and a long tail. Once it appeared, I directed it back to check up on the students who were out on their solo. As you may recall, it was at this exact time that Harvey thought he saw a bird. At any rate, it was good that I had the power to return it, or it may have attacked other people or frightened them. Creatures from a different dimension can be very unpredictable.

"There are hundreds of stories every year of sightings of strange creatures, and many of them are true. When conditions are right, these beings are most likely to appear, and most commonly this is when natural forces are in flux, such as during storms or fogs. It is at these times that it is easiest for such things to slip through from a nearby reality. Therefore, it is important that you be aware of this potential danger when you work with gateways, so you can keep these beings from coming in or can send them back or control them while they are here. Likewise, you must be careful to seal the gateway up when you are done."

Michael went on to the next danger.

"The second major danger," he observed, "is a loss of energy. It takes a great deal of power and vital energy to walk into a gateway, and if one is at an insufficient level to begin with, the drain of energy when an individual steps fully out into another dimension can cause a collapse, or even death. However, you need not be concerned with your upcoming experience," he added, sensing my uneasiness, "since this type of danger only occurs with a full gateway. The gateways we work with are not full ones and will require less power."

Michael proceeded to explain. "The first and easiest type of gateway is the working gateway. This is just a small one created by a shaman or sorcerer in conjunction with a working of magic through his focused will and energy. It is typically used for astral projection, sending spirit guides through to gain information, or to communicate with or bring through small spirits. The shaman doesn't extend any part of his body through this type of gateway.

"The second type is the partial one, involving stepping into the edge of the gateway and projecting your energy through. This is the type you will be attempting tomorrow. The advantage of such a gateway is that it provides the shaman with a highly receptive space in which to work, because it opens up a direct portal into an altered reality or into another portion of this reality. You can gain a firsthand look into this reality, perhaps meet some of the beings there, or gain some information while in this receptive state. As with the smaller gateway, you can project your consciousness astrally through time and space.

"Then, finally..." Michael paused, and looked very somber. He chose his words carefully. "...there is the full gateway. It is the most exciting, and yet the most dangerous. Only a very few shamans have attempted this successfully." He indicated that both he and Paul had done so, but only once each, because "this is not something you undertake lightly. It's like passing a great feat of endurance, but after a shaman has done it, generally once is enough.

Greta and I looked at him silently, expectantly, and Michael went on to explain. "Essentially, this gateway involves penetrating into another reality to such an extent that an individual is able to walk completely through the gateway out of this time and space, and transport himself fully into another reality or plane of existence. If you are watching, you can actually see the person disappear...

"But as I say, it's very difficult and dangerous. It requires incredible focus and power. You need every ounce of energy you can get, and it takes years of effort to build yourself up to this point, or it can be hard to survive the expenditure of energy required to go out there and then come back."

"What's a typical experience of another dimension like?" Greta wondered.

"That's hard to say. The other realities various shamans enter are so different. But I can tell you about mine." Michael went on to describe his experience at that same encampment he had just talked about, but this occurred the first night, before I had arrived.

"I started out by cutting my gateway into my double, and not into the ether or space, which is more usual. The double is a ghost-like afterimage that commonly appears near or behind a person, and cutting into it makes for a very powerful opening, because I am cutting into that part of my spirit essence that manifests as a separate figure. This double becomes visible during many magical acts and can be separated from the body. This was my focus, and cutting into it opened a gateway into myself as well as another reality, so the experience was especially intense. After the cutting, I walked out from my circle along a line of energy I had previously projected out and stepped into this gateway. Then I went through it, into an altered reality.

"Once I was there, I found myself standing on a black, obsidian plane. It was like a long, barren, rocky field that stretched out to the horizon and looked like a sheet of chipped and pitted obsidian. In the distance, I saw a whitish light glowing on the horizon. There were no stars in the sky, and it was dark except for the light.

"Then, I experienced the sensation of being completely alone, and in my aloneness I noticed to either side, and slightly behind me, a fog-like substance that enveloped me, intensifying the loneliness. With this sense of stark desolation, I turned and walked out of the gateway, and I returned to this physical reality. I sealed the gateway, and it was over. But within moments, I collapsed on the ground, totally drained of energy. I could barely move. I was shaking, and for awhile, I felt as if I was going to die. It took about two hours to recover, the experience had been so draining. To the observers, I simply walked into a foggy cloud and then vanished completely, until I returned."

We had no more questions, so Michael continued with his list of dangers.

"Now, another gateway danger is getting lost and not being able to return. Especially after a hard passage, the shaman may not be able to find the hole to return through. This has been reported by many Indian shamans, and there are even legends of whole tribes going into other worlds and not returning.

"Another danger can occur if the shaman lacks focus or experiences a sudden faltering of the will. Then, he can slip sideways through time, getting lost in the shadow world. He would disappear, without enough power to return, and would just cease to exist, lost in infinity. I have learned of this by speaking to other shamans who pass down these stories.

"Examples of the use of gateways can be found in age-old literature. For example, the Native American groups who use the *kiva* as a meditation circle, talk about using this approach to pass through gateways. The shaman uses the very center of the *kiva* as a place to project his spirit through to enter the underworld. And you can find this in Siberian shamanism. Even in Tibetan Buddhism, the monks use the mandala as a focus to concentrate in order to open a gateway into the other world.

"The two main precautions of gateway work is to accumulate the personal power needed for the work and to have a perfectly focused intent, so you can not only create or enter the gateway, but can get back."

With that, Michael turned to the illustration of a gateway on his blackboard, which depicted an hourglass-like figure on its side, with the two wide ends and the middle pinched in like two interlocked cones joined in the middle. "This illustration more accurately reflects a gateway, because going through just doesn't involve going into an opening through a passage and coming out an exit as many people think. There is some linear travel from the beginning of the gateway to the point where it disappears into another dimension, because in this reality, linear time and space exist. However, at the point at which the gateway passes into the next dimension," he said, while pointing to the pinched middle point, "the entrance has been drawn down into infinity, and then, this infinity expands immediately outward. The energy projected to the gateway reappears directly on the other side or at the exit of the gateway, having transcended all time and space. Whatever goes in one end comes out the other in an instant, because time and space no longer exists at this point of transition.

"Although this is a hard concept to explain, what it means is that the ends of the gateway could be miles or light years apart. Yet the amount of time for the willed energy to leave one end and appear on the other is virtually non-existent. What we have is a kind of artificially or naturally created black hole in space. In this area, the concentration of energy is so great that it nearly reaches the point of infinity, and then it is immediately passed through and simultaeously appears at another point in the universe.

Now, the point of infinity cannot be experienced directly, and should not be looked for, since there is a real danger that the individual trying this might lose his focus and slip into an adjacent reality. The correct way to go through a gateway is to go straight through. But it is possible to get vectored off if there is any disturbance of focus or concentration in going through the center of these two interlocked cones, representing the two planes of reality—this and the other one. However, this danger is only of concern for full gateways. For partial gateways, your only concern is that a loss of focus will result in your projection of energy or consciousness not getting through the gateway, so your work will be ineffective."

"How do you achieve this focus?" I asked.

"Through your focused will and intention," Michael answered. "You need this to create a gateway by cutting into the ether or space. And you need to maintain this focused will and intention when you project your energy through it. Let me explain the basics."

He drew a picture of a circle to the left of the inverted cones forming the hourglass shape, and next he drew a line from the center of the circle to the center of the left bottom of the sideways hourglass.

"Now, to start," he continued, "the shaman will normally set up a basic working circle, as indicated by this circle. Then, he will raise his energy to the appropriate level, and at this point, he will begin to actually cut the gateway. As he does, the area around the gateway will become foggy, and as this foggy substance continues to gather, it will become more and more dense.

"It's a general practice for the shaman making the gateway to extend some fibers of his will, which look like whitish, luminous strands, from his solar plexus outward into the gateway and then through to the other side. These fibers create a line of transmission, linking the shaman's circle and the gateway, which the shaman works with. He creates these fibers in making a partial or a full gateway by breathing or willing them out, or, he might draw a line of energy with his power object or his will from the limits of his circle along the ground to and through the gateway. Here, the line would not be connected to his solar plexus, but is just projected from his circle as part of his visualizing and willing the circle into being. Either approach can be used, depending upon style and personal choice. Or, a shaman could use both if he wanted to. Whatever is used, however, a constant visualization of the circle and its link to the gateway is necessary.

"It requires a great deal of focus to maintain the visualization of this line to the gateway and then walk out to it to whatever lies behind it. Therefore, this focused intention is critical. Otherwise, the whole structure created could easily collapse.

"Then, holding this visualization, the shaman walks out along the line he has created, or, if he has projected out fibers, these fibers will pull him in like a winch. However, the fibers are usually reserved for a full gateway. In partial gateways, which you will be doing, a line works just fine and does not require that much will or energy.

"Now, the working gateway is even simpler," he said. "It's just a focused hole into another space either through a mirror or in space. It doesn't require a circle or a line, and you don't need to walk. Rather, you project your energy to the hole and aim it to where you want it to go. Later, if you want, a working gateway can always be converted to a partial or full one by making it bigger."

Finally, Michael spoke about the methods and the importance of closing up any gateway we create after we were finished.

"You must close up when you're through, because you don't want to leave openings around for other things to get through. You are responsible for cleaning up afterwards for any magical openings or projections of energy you have created.

"The most common approach is to use a sealing motion after you have backed out or have finished your work. You just imagine yourself smoothing the gateway shut until you feel it close. You can use the side of your hand or a knife. In addition, I combine this with a banishing pentagram to seal the entry or exit slit in the gateway shut, although you can use any banishing image. I use my hand, a power object, or a visualization alone to create this image either before or after I do the sealing. Finally, I project my will or intention to see the gateway collapsing in on itself while I am doing these things, until it is firmly sealed. All of these steps are important. In fact, you may need to do these procedures several times to be sure it is closed.

"As an example, it's simply irresponsible to leave a gateway open," Michael emphasized. "Besides the possibility of letting other beings in, this is a place where there is great, concentrated energy, and where the spatial disruption could widen. It could have a serious negative affect on people. It could affect time, space, and the perception of things.

"It could create strange, psychic appearances, or, a person might suddenly vanish at this point. There have even been reports of whole towns vanishing. I had my own experience with a Safeway, which Paul and I passed when we were traveling along a freeway. You described it in your first book, and as you may recall, when we were there, the people seemed very strange, almost ghostly. When we drove back to find it later on, it wasn't there. With gateways, all sorts of bizarre events are possible, and that is why you want to close them up when you are done."

Michael had one further complication he wanted to add to his model of gateways. A gateway might exist alone, but it could also be interconnected with other gateways.

"You see," he observed, "the model of the collapsing cones is an easy way to explain the basic process. But in reality, there are multiple-linked gateways, with passageways all over from one dimension to the next. That's why your focus is so important. Without it, you could easily end up coming in or going out of the wrong gateway.

"Then, too," he added with an impish grin, "that infinite point in the middle of gateways exists as a theoretical link, but at the same time, it does not really exist, because when the entrances and exits are joined, there is no intervening time and space. This is the essential paradox. They exist in time and space on one level when we work with them, but at the same time, we transcend space and time also. This can be mind-boggling to think about. It seems as if the universe is playing with us with these paradoxes. Yet, the advanced shaman can rise above all this, for through his understanding of paradoxes and through his work, he can step out of ordinary time and space to move between the multiple dimensions of reality that exist in the world.

Greta was satisfied with the explanation, commenting on her life's experiences with disappearances, reappearances, and strange beings she noticed on night drives, but I looked at Michael with deep puzzlement. He addressed his remarks to me.

"Think about the gateways you may have encountered in your own life. Notice what strange and anomalous things might have happened. Consider: could it have been a gateway? Maybe so. Maybe not. The point is to pay attention, be aware, and realize the potential around us."

And on that note, Michael announced it was time to take a break. When we came back, we would learn about mirrors and their use to create gateways. Then he added some thoughts for for me to think about: "Just remember the line from Hamlet: 'There are more things than are dreamt of in your philosophy.' Gateways are like that—strange but true. You need to believe in their existence in order to work with them and open the doors to new realities."

# CHAPTER ELEVEN

## LEARNING ABOUT WORK WITH MIRRORS

After about twenty minutes, Michael invited us to come back to the living room. He was ready to start the next lesson on working with mirrors. "You'll need your own mirror for this," he told me, and I got out the mirror Michael had bought me for this purpose. It was about 9" x 12" in a white plastic frame, and still in its plastic shrink-packed wrapping from the drug store. I removed the wrapping before we started.

As Michael began the lesson, I noticed the large mirror which he used, covered by a black velvet slip cover and propped up on the blackboard beside him. He began.

"Mirrors are an ideal tool for working with gateways. The magical property of mirrors has long been known." He gave some examples from history and legend, including the story in which the prince uses a magic mirror to help him find his sleeping princess.

"The reason for their popularity is that they let a person see through them into other realities and then step into these realities. This is accomplished through the use of the reflective surface, and water could serve the same purpose. You must first properly charge and activate the surface, and you need the ability to be able to look.

"There is also some danger in the use of mirrors, since once a mirror is activated, this creates a two-way gateway, so you can not only reach through and project your own energy through it, but anything on the other side can likewise reach through and project at you. When we talked about the possibility of something coming through partial and full gateways, we were talking about a product of the shaman's focused will, and in that case, the shaman has more control over the movement through the gateway, since it is his own creation. By contrast, mirrors possess a natural two-way quality due to their surface qualities, and since all mirrors can be gateways, any mirror can be linked to any other. So a shaman can project into one mirror, and from there, out of any other mirror. Thus the mirror presents the risk of anything on the other side reaching through and projecting to you. This is a form of gateway to gateway transmission, and it happens instantaneously. You can use windows for this purpose, too. Now, a shaman can create an entrance or an exit to a gateway anywhere using his will. But a mirror is more efficient, because it is especially conductive. Furthermore, the properties of any two mirrors is the same, so it is easy to enter and exit through any set of mirrors, because there's less energy needed to pass from gateway to gateway. That's because the level of energy doesn't have to be modified in moving from one type of object to another."

"Why would different substances have this effect?" I asked.

"Because all matter is composed of energy of different vibrations or frequencies. As a result, when you project your energy through different mediums, such as water, glass, or air, it goes through with a slightly different frequency, so subtle that you may not even notice it. But movement between the substances will mean slightly altering the energy rate. However with two mirrors, like other gateways of the same medium, this is not necessary, and the process is more efficient."

Michael glanced over his list of things to talk about.

"Okay, now let me tell you a little about some of the dangers you may confront in your work with mirrors, so you'll know what precautions to take.

"One of the common dangers is encountering entities from other dimensions. In fact, one of the most common examples of this is the ritual of evoking Bloody Mary out of the mirror, which is something many kids do. I've had many people tell me they have done this as children. The kids gather in a dark room and gaze into the mirror, while chanting the name Bloody Mary and visualizing a being representing her showing up. In almost every case I heard about, something weird happens. Usually, it's an old woman covered with blood, something that frightens the kids enough not to repeat the experiment. Maybe this imaage of Bloody Mary started out as a product of their imagination, but after years of gathering energy from enough of this concentrated effort, a certain form has grown. Now it is much easier to evoke her, just as it is much easier for her to step through a mirror, if the gateway is left open or if a person working with a mirror loses control. Much the same process might occur with any entity that is given energy by being called up again and again over time."

Michael went on to another item on his list. "Another possible danger involves reactivating a gateway in a mirror if you are sloppy in closing it when you are done. If a mirror is not fully closed, it can start transmitting again, and perhaps let something through."

"How can you tell if the mirror isn't fully shut down?" asked Greta.

"One way to tell is if the mirror still feels warm, a property of the mirror when it is functioning. Also, you may notice the surface becoming luminous, or taking on a rippling, fluid quality, a little like liquid mercury, so that the reflections are no longer sharp, but instead appear fuzzy and vibrating. The energy drawn into the mirror creates these effects, and the warmth of the mirror is one of the surest indicators that the gateway is currently active. If you still feel warmth after closing a gateway, you need to do more to close it up."

He then moved on to the possible uses of mirrors.

"First, you can use the mirror as a focusing tool for your astral projection. Also, you can use a mirror for communication. For example, you can send a message to another person who is receiving through astral projection, whether he is gazing into the mirror or not. Then too, mirrors are good for improving your ability to do far distant or remote viewing, because they will help you astrally travel, so you can better see distant places and events. In addition, you can use these to do divination. You simply wish to see things in the future, and watch as they appear as scenes in the mirror. These scenes emanate to you from the mirror and then are viewed in your mind's eye. The mirror is not a view screen, but a focus, so you will also be able to sense and feel these things as well. This is somewhat like a crystal ball, although they have traditionally been used to get information on the past or future. The mirror is more versatile, because of its many other uses as a gateway.

"And lastly," Michael said, "when used as a gateway, the mirror can function just like any other gateway. For example, you can focus your energy through it with a specific intent and with a specific destination in mind. Also, a shaman can call and evoke a spirit through this mirror, and he can send his familiar through his mirror to a specific location, perhaps to gather information for him without going there himself. I've used my familiar that way to obtain information on someone I was going to meet before the meeting took place. Mirrors are excellent gateways because they are so receptive, making it easy to focus, receive, and project energy through them. They are often preferred over creating gateways in open space or using any other medium."

Now, his general introduction over, Michael asked me to get my own mirror. "It has to be specially prepared, stored, and used to become a magic mirror used for magical purposes," he said.

He took out a small piece of cloth about the size of a dish rag and asked me to hand him my mirror.

"First of all," he explained, "the mirror should be clean," and he demonstrated how I should rub the mirror carefully with a piece of cloth to remove any bits of dust, fingerprints, or other dirt.

"Then too, it should be new or exorcised thoroughly, so that no vibrations from any previous owner can intrude. You want to make it completely your own, and you want to keep it that way through proper care and cleaning."

Michael motioned for me to come and stand beside him in front of the coffee table upon which he had placed various ritual items—a small dish of salt, a metal chalice with water, an incense burner.

"Now we'll go over exorcising the mirror," he said. "First, you want to charge your salt and water and then combine the two." He asked me to send energy first to the salt and then to the water to charge them. Then, I put a small pinch of salt into the water, as he instructed. Next, he asked me to charge the incense, which I did by looking at it intently and imagining my energy going out to it.

Michael went on. "Okay, now take your salt water and sprinkle it over the surface of the item you are purifying. The salt water acts as a demagnetizer and neutralizes the psychic charges held in the object. Any object can hold a charge, and you want to get rid of this.

"Now that you have done this..." he pointed to the small drops of water I had sprinkled on the glass, "visualize the energy of this water interacting with the energy field of the object, and see them both disrupting the energies held within it and releasing them." I answered okay when I had done this.

"Then take the mirror and pass it through the charged incense smoke, so that you expose the entire object to the smoke." When I had completed this, he went on, "Once you have finished this and you feel the object is free and clear of any previous vibrations or energies, you want to charge it with your own energy by infusing it with your own power, just as you would in charging any object. Visualize the energy coming through your body, and using your breath, bring the energy out through your arms and hands into the object. Meanwhile, as you do this, see yourself infusing this object with all of your energy and power." I indicated to him when I had completed this task.

"Okay, now," Michael said, "use your seeing exercises to determine the extent to which your energy has penetrated the object. The more brilliant the energy field around the object appears, the more interpenetrated the object has been. If the field looks very bright and shimmery, that's fine. But if it seems a little dull, then charge it some more."

I wasn't sure, so I focused on charging the mirror for about another minute.

"Okay, that's good enough," Michael commented, and I released the charge.

Then, putting the mirror down on the table, I asked, "Why is it necessary to exorcise this mirror, since it's already new?'

"It's a good idea to do this exorcism as a routine, even if the mirror is new, because it has been handled by others before you obtained it."

Michael excused himself, went into another room for a few moments, and came back with a pillowcase with light blue flowers. He motioned for me to place the mirror into it.

"Once you've charged your mirror, you want to put it in a cloth bag to keep it away from the light until you use it. The mirror is very sensitive to the energy of the light, and this energy could overcharge your mirror. You want to be in control of the amount of energy your mirror possesses. This bag was something I had around, but you can get your own cover. The best covering is one made of black satin or a similar material, so a minimum of light reaches it. If it is a hanging mirror, use a drape. Some people also put mirrors in a trunk.

"Besides keeping the mirror protected from the light, this covering also protects it, according to an old belief that you must be careful of what the mirror sees. You don't want to leave it exposed and open to energies or emanations that you don't want your mirror to pick up. This is an old belief of the traditional European witches, as well as the modern European and Oriental shamans who work with mirrors.

"Now, a few more points about exposing your mirror. Another belief is that once a mirror is opened up, activated, and used in a particular place, that place can be discovered by other individuals who are focusing through that gateway. Perhaps nothing would happen, but then, perhaps the magician could look in on the person using the mirror or direct some negative energy against him. Therefore, keeping your mirror covered helps to minimize the things that are visible where you are.

"Also, you want to be sure to seal up your mirror when you are finished using it. Unless you do, your mirror will retain something of the impression of whatever it sees; so potentially someone else could pick this up off your mirror later, or the lingering energy might interfere with your future seeing. The process works a little like psychometry. Any object can gain an impression of the things that affect it, but a mirror is more sensitive. So, you want to seal it to prevent the unwanted entrance of other magical activities, such as far distant viewing. Also, you want to avoid leaving the mirror out if it is still activated, because then  someone passing by can see into it, or one can look into it through projection, since, if the mirror is still open, someone can look into the mirror from far away."

"How can you tell it's active now?" I asked.

"You'll notice quite a bit of activity near the chair. Just look and you'll see a kind of smoking haze and some sparkles of energy."

"Yes, I can see that very clearly," Greta commented.

"So that means the mirror can be used as a gazing focus or a gateway, since it is ready to work."

After we gazed at the mirror for a few minutes, Michael made a few brushing and thrusting motions with his hands.

"Now, this is another way of sealing the mirror," he said. "You can also seal it up without the use of a formal seal by simply visualizing it sealed, or by using a sealing pentagram like I'm using now or any other image you associate with sealing. It's a little more effective if you go through the physical motions of sealing it up, as you visualize and project the intention that the mirror is now sealed. If you attempt this with your mind's eye alone, your energy will tend to dissipate. So you have a stronger focus when you seal it physically."

When he was done, he asked us to put our hands in front of the mirror, each in turn.

"You see, the surface is cool now. And you no longer see all those sparkles of energy. The mirror is now deactivated, and it is like an ordinary mirror, although you don't want to use it as an ordinary mirror. Nor do you want to leave it exposed even after it is sealed. This is a powerful tool, and it would not focus as well if it were used for mundane purposes. Besides, you might also pick up images of others who might look into it, say to comb their hair or adjust a hat, and you certainly don't want that. It would destroy the magic of the mirror by turning it into something mundane."

Michael put his mirror away and then pointed to a black ceramic bowl on the table. There was what looked like the image of a sculptured woman with long hair bending over one side of the bowl, and it was filled with about two inches of water.

"This is another version of a magic mirror," he explained. "It can be filled with water or not. And it can be used much like a mirror as a gazing surface or a gateway. The major difference is that this is a bowl rather than a reflective surface. The concave shape of the bowl and the quality of the water help to determine the experience of what you see. So it's generally a less intense, gentler, more diffuse type of experience."

"Why is it painted black?" Greta wanted to know.

"It's black and has some small white dots representing stars to give it a feeling of the night sky. This helps to give it a more powerful focus. Also, besides painting a bowl, you could use one made out of a black stone. Paul has one made out of obsidian that is very, very powerful."

I bent down to look at the bowl more closely, and as I touched it, Michael pulled it away. "Generally, you don't want others to touch these items," he admonished me, "because you don't want to mingle others' energies with your own. These objects are more powerful if they are responsive just to us."

He took a cloth and wiped the bowl off. Then, he brushed it a few times and recharged it with his own energy. "For optimal performance," he emphasized, "you want the item to respond only to you."

"But you've let others use your staff," I said, not understanding why Michael should be especially careful about this.

"That's different," he answered. "It's a less finely tuned object. A power object for general use does not require such stringent care. But mirrors and gazing bowls are more sensitive; so you need to employ more protections to keep the energy in the bowl your own, and to keep other energies out. However," Michael added, "you can use either special or ordinary materials to make such a bowl. The important thing is to prepare it for use like the mirror, by first exorcising and charging it. Then it is ready to be used as a focus."

Michael was ready to show me how to use my mirror, so I removed it from its case. He asked me to position it so it sat up, and I placed it against the back of a chair near the fireplace. "We're going to do an exercise now in which you'll do some gazing and flying using the mirror as a focus."

I stood in front of the mirror and looked down into it. "Flying?" I said.

"A kind of astral projection," he answered. "But you'll have the experience of flying."

Michael dimmed the lights, so there was only a single candle glowing. As I continued to look into the mirror, he moved away from me and sat on the couch.

"Now, I'd like you to use the same unfocused gaze as when you do your seeing. You must look past your reflection into the depth of the mirror."

Then he fell silent for a few minutes. I gazed ahead, letting my eyes go out of focus, so that the image in front of me began to go blurry. At first it was hard to see past it.

"Just let the image of yourself go," I heard Michael saying from far away. "Don't pay attention to it. Just let your seeing project out through your mind's eye, allowing nothing in your reflection to distract you. You must see yourself going through the mirror. Just let your gaze penetrate deep within until you are not even there."

Finally, in a very trancey, spacey state, I nodded to indicate that I had done this.

"Okay, now you are ready to fly," he said, in a thin and distant voice. I nodded once more, and he continued very softly in a monotone voice. "See yourself as a point of consciousness traveling through the mirror... You are up in the sky... You can see the cool, dark, night air around you... Just feel yourself flying through it... Now you are experiencing yourself coming down towards San Francisco... You can see the pyramid shape of the Transamerica Building ahead of you... Now you are circling around it..." Now I could feel myself soaring, as if I were high up in the air looking down on the city, while his voice went on.

"And from here you are flying on to your own house... Now you are on the street outside... Just look around... Feel yourself flying up and down the street... Then, you can fly into your house briefly... You can see yourself going like light through the window... And then you can look around for a few moments... Now, feeling complete and ready to return, you can fly out... Very quickly you are on your way back... Now you are flying over the streets of Beverly Hills... Finally, you are returning back into the house, and back into the room."

After I took a minute or so to readjust to being back, Michael wanted to know how the experience felt.

"I felt myself soaring, like I wasn't here at all," I commented. "I saw myself flying up above the places you mentioned, and then when I was in my house, I looked around to make sure everything was locked, and if the answering machine was still on. It seemed to be."

"Well, you will find that your seeing is usually pretty accurate when you fly like this, although that wasn't the purpose of this exercise. I just wanted you to experience traveling through the mirror and flying. Did you experience anything else?"

I thought for a moment. "Well, I felt a little coldness or maybe a draft in the air as I was standing there."

"Yes, that's common," he remarked. "There's a tendency to experience the phenomena of going into the mirror this way, because you are in effect passing into the colder region of space. This is common when going through a gateway to somewhere else. Now, place your hand near the center of the mirror, but don't touch it. What do you feel?"

"It feels a little warm," I said.

"Exactly," Michael replied. "It feels warm because it has been very energized by your working with it and going through it. Now, since you are finished, I want you to seal it. Use the sealing pentagram I showed you and then brush your hands across it, as if you are sending the energy away. Do it a few times, until the mirror feels cool again and is really sealed."

I did so, and Michael put his hand across the mirror to check. It still felt a little warm to him, so I repeated the motions a few more times. When he rechecked, it felt sealed to him, and he told me to put it away in its case.

I did so and then Michael answered my last question about the difference between this traveling and doing geo-teleportation or conscious projection.

"The main difference is that traveling through the mirror is more intense and there is more clarity. It's more accurate because you are using a gateway, and not just imaging your consciousness traveling through space. Also, you are more conscious and in control, because you have to hold that strong focus needed to travel through the mirror. In conscious projection, since you need less focus and control, the experience tends to be more diffuse."

He then handed me two small, white candles and gave me my homework. "I'd like you to go on a few guided trips of your own. Decide in advance where you are headed, or tape the journey as you did tonight. Then, go on your trip while you listen. Use candles for lighting. You want to do this in a dark, quiet place. Notice if you experience any problems, and be aware of the sharpness of your sensations. Also notice how it feels to pass through the mirror. And don't try to visit or look on anyone with magical ability, since they may have blocks or protections set up. Or you could encounter familiars or some strange being, which would disrupt your trip because you won't know what to do."

"Okay," I agreed.

"Finally," Michael warned, "if you do encounter any problems or feel uncomfortable doing this, pull out and come back through the mirror. Avoid hostile situations because your travel has been through a two-way hole, and you are vulnerable to anyone you encounter projecting anything back. They can project energy back into the mirror at you, and you might get hit with it. Stay away from anything negative."

"How long should I practice this?" I wondered.

"Perhaps ten to twenty minutes, or as long as you feel comfortable," Michael advised. "When you are done, seal the mirror and put it away, because you have created a small gateway, and it must be completely closed when you through. You may need a few tries to shut it, but just check by putting your hand over the surface to feel any warmth. No warmth means that it's closed."

Finally, Michael reminded me to do my regular energy raising exercises to stimulate my pineal gland, and to raise up the colors through my chakras, emphasizing their importance since I would be expending a great amount of energy when I projected myself through the mirror. The energy raising exercises would keep me from being drained, and they would help me to see more, do more, and have a better trip. I promised I would do as he recommended and said goodnight. There was much to think about as I drove back to the hotel.

# CHAPTER TWELVE

## WORKING WITH GATEWAYS

Back at the hotel, I was eager to try out the mirror technique I had just learned. I set the mirror on a chair next to the bed, and sat in another chair across from it. I lit one of the candles Michael had given me. As I gazed into the mirror, I ignored my own reflection. In a few moments my face faded into blackness, and I found myself swooping up and down the streets of Los Angeles, seeing things from a bird's eye point of view.

"Where should I go?" I wondered to myself, and I thought of a friend from twenty years ago, whose address I had found on a map, in the hills above Hollywood. I made my way there, flying down the freeway and up into the hills. I could make out the houses perched in the darkness in the canyons, and then I was there.

I circled around a split level white stucco house between two other houses festooned with Christmas lights, and came in closer. I peered into the windows, hovering, and yet standing almost motionless in space. The house was dark, but I could make out what appeared to be a den. I hesitated a moment, and then went in. It was odd to be there, and momentarily, I felt a rush of self-consciousness, and decided to proceed cautiously, as if my being there was somehow creating a physical presence that someone could sense. I moved through the rooms, getting strong and clear impressions of the furniture and environment, which seemed to indicate someone living alone.

But then, in the kitchen, I suddenly realized there was no one here. The refrigerator was bare, and on the table I noticed a note to the property manager taking care of the home. There were instructions on taking messages from the answering machine and on watering the plants, and I realized that he was away for the holidays.

I turned and flew out of the house and back to my mirror. In a moment, I breathed in my consciousness and was back in my own head again, looking at my shadowy reflection in the dark mirror. Everything had seemed so real, but was it so? I would have to try to check it out somehow.

Then, I sealed the gateway in the mirror with the brushing and banishing motions Michael had taught me, and put it back in its case.

The next evening, after a day of writing and a brief break to run on the beach, I was back at Michael's again. No one else had arrived yet, since Michael had said he wanted to work privately with me to do some demonstrations.

"We'll go out on the lawn in the backyard," he said. "I want to show you how to make some small gateways yourself, and then you'll have a chance to practice, so you'll be ready to make and enter your big one on Friday."

It was a chill, moonlit night as we went out, and I put on my heavy, black down jacket and gloves. I noticed the nearly full moon just above the towering pine tree at the edge of the lawn.

"I'll start by demonstrating what you'll do first," Michael said. "Then you can try."

He strode out to the center of the lawn, dressed completely in black too, and holding his long staff by his side as a power object.

"Remember what I was saying about gateways," he told me firmly before he began. "You must not only build it right, but you must have the destination you ultimately intend to reach clearly in your mind. This way, as you project your energy through the gateway, you are also picturing that energy passing very clearly through the gateway to your destination and reaching it."

"Yes, I remember," I nodded.

"Good," he said. "Now..." He turned ninety degrees to face down the lawn towards the pine tree and raised his staff in the air "we'll start with a simple working gateway, which is very basic. You want to start by focusing your seeing in the air in front of you. Then, using an appropriate power object like this staff or your own hands, you want to project the energy out from the tip of your power object or hands. Then visualize it cutting the energy of the air in front of you to carve a hole into the scene in front of you..." He slashed his staff down as he said this. "And now the energy goes through the hole and into space. Notice how the quality of the energy directly in front of me changes, and that there is definitely a slit."

I saw a few sparkles of energy in a row. Michael was satisfied and went on. "Okay. Now I'm going to picture myself widening this slit to create a working space." He moved his hands in a series of broad, cupping motions. "I am moving my power object down and around to create a cone shape. As I do, I visualize my energy penetrating through the layers of the ether or atmosphere around this area and from that point into space. I gaze at that point the way I taught you to gaze into the mirror, so what I am really looking at is the hole I have produced, and not the scene in front of me. I project my consciousness and my will in, and visualize this hole as a gateway into another space. I believe this is a door. I must believe that."

He paused, and I let his words sink in. Then, he announced, "Okay, now I'm going to send an energy dart through the gateway."

Holding his power object in the crook of his hand, he rubbed his hands together in a broad, rolling motion, like kneading dough, to create an energy dart. Holding it in one hand and pushing with the other, he sent it to the gateway, and announced that it had disappeared. I asked where it had gone.

"No one knows where," Michael continued, "because the space I visualized was simply open space, so the energy dart could be anywhere in there. But now, I'll be a little more specific, and I'll focus my attention so that the end of the gateway occurs somewhere else." He looked around, and settled on a point directly ahead of me, about two feet above the lawn, in the middle of a small bush.

"I'll have the dart come out here," he pointed, "and there are two ways I can do this. I can visualize the dart coming out at that spot. But, in a more forceful and controlled approach, I can visualize what it would look like to see the dart come out from that gateway, by looking from that direction myself. I just visualize myself there and looking out. In this case, I'll walk over to the site I have selected and take a look. Or I could have imagined I was here by projecting my consciousness. Looking at what happens to the dart helps to visualize the energy coming out."

He walked to the small bush in front of me and turned to face the original gateway he had made. He moved his hands to widen it once more, since a few minutes had passed, and he felt the energy around the opening had coalesced together in spots.

"Okay, now, keeping that vision of the exit gateway in mind," he continued, "I'm going to shoot energy through the first gateway...and now it's going right past you and..." he whirled around slightly, "...it goes into that grove right there. Did you see anything?" I reported seeing some sparkling. He wanted me to watch more closely as he threw a more powerful dart, that also zoomed out and flew across the lawn. "Where did it land?" he asked, but I wasn't able to tell him. He laughed. "You really have to look. The energy won't always be where you expect, and you need to learn to work with your seeing, not your expectations."

He rolled one last dart and sent it in a circle around me. I felt a slight pressure in the air around me, and he was satisfied when I reported this. "That's fine," he said, "you don't have to see anything. You can feel things as well, and that pressure around your waist is exactly where I sent the energy dart, so that suggests you were really picking something up."

Michael walked towards the gateway and motioned for me to follow. "Well, that was a small example, involving visualizing a location and putting energy through. You can look at the gateway more closely, but don't go into it yet." He pointed with his staff. "Notice how it's hanging in space." I looked where he pointed. There seemed to be a few faint sparkles of light in front of us. "To see it better, I'll stimulate it with my power object," he went on. "There's a very definite feeling of energy here. In fact, it's traveling straight down in a kind of a cone shape away from me to a point in space here.

"Now, you can experience how it feels yourself. So just walk ahead with me a few steps, and put your hand out. Then, feel into the cone at that dark spot right ahead, and notice that it feels colder in there, and then warmer as you pull your hand away again."

I tried the process several times and nodded.

"Well, that's the cone," Michael exhorted. "You're feeling the cone of the gateway, and that's the point where you're in that infinite point of nothingness. That's why it's somewhat colder there. You have touched the void."

We stepped back, and he proceeded to seal the gateway by stabbing at the patch of energy with his staff. He mentioned the importance of not leaving a gateway open so that things from the other side could get through, and said that it required only basic sealing to evaporate it. Residues of scattered energy particles didn't matter.

Next, he pointed ahead about fifteen feet on the lawn, and explained that he was going to create a larger, partial gateway that was human size. He made his circle, brought up his energy, reached out through space, and cut the gateway.

"Now notice the rippling effect as I bring my staff down," he said, "and notice that the quality of light at that end has changed to a goldish color. That's because the energy there is stronger, more intense. And nearby, you'll notice how the energy is gathering as a kind of foggy mist."

I nodded, indicating that I though I could see it getting foggy in this area of more intense energy.

Michael continued. "All right. Now I will widen the gateway, picturing and drawing an oval shape with my staff. The energy radiating around the oval looks like a tunnel, which is the cone forming into the other dimension." He made a few more circles in the air with his staff. "Now I'm extending that tunnel wall towards me, and I'm extending the energy line from my circle outward to connect with the tunnel.

"Then, I walk out along the line I drew" he continued as he walked, "while I maintain my focus on the gateway. It widens, and then I'm right up to the edge of it. I could continue on in, or I could bring a being through."

I glanced at Michael surprised. "A being?"

"Yes, I can bring through a particular energy form, although, in this case, I'm going to call on my familiar, as you'll later learn how to do. You bind a particular being to you to help in your spiritual work.

"You can see that little luminous area at the end of the gateway. That's my familiar. She appeared in the triangle of manifestation I created near the gate, and then she stepped into the gateway. When I beckon her out, she goes there..." he said, pointing to a bush about fifteen feet at the edge of the lawn, "...and now there...she's coming back... You can see the luminous ball of energy as she goes."

At this point, I was seeing so many sparkles and flashes of light all around the lawn, that I wasn't sure what I was seeing.

Finally, Michael announced that his familiar was back in the gateway, and he was sending her back. He breathed the energy line back in, closed up his circle, and scattered the energy of the gateway again. He wanted to know what I saw, and I told him I had observed a whitish line from his circle, and a glowing energy around him, which appeared foggy as he moved into the area where he created the gateway. He indicated that these were typical images.

"The radiance you saw around me is the force coming out of the gateway itself. I was seeing and feeling the line to this oval hole I created, as well as imagining the luminous edges, and beyond that, just space. I didn't visualize any end to the thing. You were picking up my visualization itself, because our thoughts all create energy, which has a physical impression out there. When you learn to see, you can see that also, and you can create that too in your own magical acts."

As we compared experiences, he pointed out one difference that was quite common. "When people see me going into the gateway, it does usually look foggy, and as I come out, they usually report seeing me clearly, as if I am stepping back into everyday reality, which you also reported. But for me, the sensation is just the opposite. I think that's because we are perceiving from different realities. I'm seeing the other reality on the other side of the gateway clearly as I step into it, although I am seeing your reality foggy when I return and am still adjusting. By contrast, since you are perceiving from the real world, I appear foggy when I leave your reality, and then I become clear again when I return to it.

"Anyway, once I'm back out of the gateway, the rest of the return is easy, I enter back into the circle, and quickly clean up the energy of the gateway and the circle. So now do you think you are ready to try this yourself?"

I nodded, and went to get my staff. As Michael stood on the patio, I walked to the center of the lawn and made a circle around myself, since Michael said I could make a circle or not in making a simple gateway and I preferred to do so. It helped me feel I was going to be doing a special magical act. Then, lifting my staff, I visualized a small oval gateway forming in the air before me as I cut it. Michael instructed me to push in the hole and make it more cone shaped, while focusing until it came to a very fine point. I was amazed at his precision, as if he could see the very thoughts I projected, and I tried to concentrate more intently on the image I was trying to form.

"Now, visualize that point getting finer and finer," he went on, "until it literally passes through the scene you are looking at and into space. Picture it passing through the gateway into a dark space beyond... Now give it a little more definition, although be gentle... Push down a little more, and give it some energy, and charge it."

Finally, he was satisfied with the gateway I had created, and I thought I saw some pulsations of light in the area, which he defined as the energy forming. He asked me to approach the area slowly to experience the coolness as I neared the cone. I moved forward, and in moments, I noticed the coolness. He told me to move a little further and notice it getting even colder. I nodded, feeling the distinct chill in the air. He then told me to return my place in the circle.

Michael now asked me to create some energy darts and send them through the gateway. I cupped my hands and rolled them back and forth to imagine the energy ball forming, and then threw it. I imagined it going into the gateway.

"Good," he observed, "and in it goes. And then it disappears."

He asked me to do this several more times and coached me as I did. "Push the dart a little more strongly this time... Picture it going through into that dark space at the end of the gateway... Then it vanishes... Don't pay any attention to the background...

Just look at this dark space and nothing else... Let the energy dart go into that cone of dark space so it disappears into nothingness."

He asked me to imagine another gateway above the trees, while I still remained conscious of the first one. Holding both gateways in mind, I was, he instructed me, to picture the energy going through the first gateway, and after a slight delay, coming out of the second one. Then, I was to visualize shooting the dart from there to a spot on the pavement about six feet away from him.

He watched as I concentrated on visualizing the pattern he described. It was a little hard to imagine at first, but finally I had created the picture, and I looked up in the air as if the energy dart I had sent in was really up there.

"And there it goes to the ground," he announced, as I imagined the dart coming down. But, he wanted me to try it once more, with more control. This time, he still wasn't satisfied, indicating that the dart was tumbling. "You want to visualize it coming straight down and not at you, but at the pavement." I was surprised he was aware of such detail. It seemed he was able to pick up the subtleties of my inner thoughts, so that if I wasn't visualizing with precision, he could actually sense this.

Finally, after several more throws, Michael was satisfied. "You see, you just have to work on focusing, and you can do it. Otherwise, these things will have a tendency to tumble. But not bad for your first time. Not bad."

Then, he suggested I use my staff instead of my visualization alone to make the process even easier.

"Just take your power object and project your energy up through it to cut a gateway up where you imagined that gateway before. You'll see the area there still glowing, since it was the focus of all this energy. Now just improve it." I raised my staff and did as he instructed.

"You see, that strengthens it," he stated. "The edges of the hole are glowing more strongly now. So now let's shoot another dart through it."

I rolled another dart as I had before and pushed it in, using my visualization as before to see it coming to the ground.

"Good," Michael exclaimed after I was done. "You see, the dart was more definite this time. It was much easier to control. And you notice how it came down a little straighter."

Then, Michael stepped over beside me to shoot through a few darts himself. "What I want to show you," he said, "is that anyone can use any gateway, once it is created. It doesn't matter who created it. The energy exists and is out there, so anyone can work with it."

He pointed to the gateway with his staff. "And now observe the state of the space up there," he said. "Notice how it's tingly and crackly." I nodded. "It will stay that way until you seal it. So close up your original gateway and then seal that one."

I moved my staff around with the banishing motions Michael had taught me.

"Good," he said, "and now it's closed. You'll notice there's no more energy coming out. The sparkling and tingling in the air around those gateways is gone."

I glanced up and down and around. The atmosphere did seem quieter.

"Does the order in which you close up the gateways matter?" I asked.

"No, not really," he replied. "But I like closing the nearest one first. It just feels neater that way."

Then he motioned for us to go back inside. The demonstration was over, and he wanted to talk about the process of projecting the will.

"We'll be learning about the luminous energy fibers you send out when you project. When the others come over, we'll do some demonstrations with mirrors and gateways. And after that, I think you'll be ready, and we'll go into the field so you can make your partial gateway and then step in."

# CHAPTER THIRTEEN

## *LEARNING ABOUT ENERGY FIBERS*

When we walked inside, I discovered that Paul, his girlfriend Sara, and Greta, had already arrived, and were waiting for us in the living room.

"They'll be helping us with the demonstration on mirrors we'll be doing next," Michael said, "and then they'll be going with us to see you make your gateway."

I sat down on the couch, and Michael took up his usual position near the blackboard to begin the lesson.

"I want to tell you about extending your luminous fibers," he began. "You can use this technique to help you in reaching in or extending yourself into your gateway if you want." He pointed to a figure on the board of a man with a bright, elongated shape, looking something like a extended snail, projecting out of his belly.

"These represent the luminous fibers which project out of the belly," he continued. "They are basically tools for extending the will; they are other ways of projecting your willed energy." He drew a picture of a circle and a mushroom-like shape next to it. "Remember when we talked about haras?" he asked me. "This is the seat of your personal power or will, and you can project your energy out of the hara or will center. You can feel this will coming out as fibers of luminous energy, and they really do extend. When someone else does such a projection, if you have the ability to see, you can actually see these fibers.

"Many people are unfamiliar with the way these fibers can extend out and be used to project the intentions of the will at great distances. Not only can these fibers be used to transmit a willed intention, but you can sense and perceive things with them too. They can be used to work with your will as well as sense things about the environment which you come into contact with. The generation of these luminous fibers is a conscious act of power. It takes time to develop the process, and they will be weak at first, because your will is not strong. But as you do this technique more and more, you will be able to project these fibers out further and further. You control these fibers directly with the breath as a willed intention, and then you project the energy of your body into these fibers, accompanied by your physical breathing."

Michael directed me to look at the close-up view of the end of the fibers. It looked like the tip of a swabbing stick dipped in oil.

"Now look closely," Michael said. "The luminescence in these fibers projects along a kind of stalk, and then it flowers out into a broader tip that is bright and luminous, a little like a match head or a squid's tentacle. So there's this bulging or flaring at the end of the fibers. Also, there may be some little side projections or flares, if the will is not so focused, so these little sparks of energy veer off to the sides. Or, these side projections may be due to the interaction of the energy in the air with these fibers. Or, it may be a combination of both.

"In short," concluded Michael, "these energy fibers consist of four basic parts—the stalk, the head, the fibers or flares which project along the stalk or off of it, and finally, the sparkles of energy which you see shooting out of these fibers and flares. These fibers come out of the individual body in varying lengths, depending upon the strength of the will and other factors. When a person isn't very well trained, these fibers tend to whip around each other in an unruly bundle, a little bit like a knot of hair that's all messed up. But they can be trained like a vine to reach out in unison to whatever the person's intended goal is. For example, the person may want to reach into a gateway to pull something out, or if he wants to pull himself inside, he can use his fibers to latch onto something to pull him in. Also, the more energy you project into these fibers, the farther they will extend, and the more luminescent and brighter they will appear.

"However," he added, "this process is not an automatic one. The fibers must be breathed out, and to get them back, you must breathe them back in. Also, once you have activated these fibers, you must be very careful, because you have to hold a grounded position for some time, and you might even experience some abdominal cramping, as a result of focusing so much energy out of the area and then whipping it around. Like working unused muscles the first time, you can get stiff."

He had a few more cautions to add. "You must be careful what these fibers come into contact with. These are connected to your hara, which is very sensitive. You will be very vulnerable to negative energy, and you must be careful of such energy. For example, you wouldn't want to touch that sacrificial stela we saw in the museum.

"Finally, you want to have a clear picture of where you are going. You don't want to leave these fibers dangling around, where they can catch onto anything and make you feel scattered. Rather, they must be willed to your destination, such as the other side of a gateway. Once they reach their target, they must be willed to wrap around or attach themselves to that intended target, or to make contact with that target if you are trying to sense something from the energy field of an object. Remember, once you project these fibers, do not lose your focus, or you will pass by or drop your target."

"I'll remember that," I assured Michael, and with that, we took a break.

# CHAPTER FOURTEEN

## *DEMONSTRATIONS WITH MIRRORS AND GATEWAYS*

"Now we're going to show you something pretty amazing," Michael announced after the break. "We'll be doing a number of experiments with mirrors and gateways to demonstrate what is really possible, once you know how to work with these. As you'll discover, our so-called ordinary reality is really a lot more fluid and permeable than most people think. You can move it and bend it as you bring in energies from other dimensions.

"First, we will create a working gateway in a mirror. Also, we'll demonstrate the Einsteinian effect, which is the transmission of energy from one mirror to another on an instantaneous basis, because you are really dealing with two gateways. We will show you how to pass a denser part of your own energy from one gateway or mirror to another, and you'll see this energy materialize out of the receiving mirror. You will learn the differences between the use of mirrors and a reflective surface by projecting energies. And, you will see how you can breathe in energy from the mirror when you go outside. All of this will help you when you create your own gateway later tonight," Michael said.

"It sounds intriguing," I said, and Michael dimmed the lights, so only a single candle lit the room.

"Now, we'll start by gazing into our own mirrors to get attuned." I asked if I needed to exorcise my mirror once again.

"No, not at all," Michael laughed. "You want to accumulate a charge in the mirror now. Not clear it out."

As we set our mirrors up, I noticed Paul's had an elongated, hexagonal shape.

"I use this shape because it suits my own energy," he explained. "It's used for special workings; you could use any type that suits you, of any kind of material or surface. I have used obsidian ones for some purposes, and there are concave and convex ones also. You can experiment as you gain experience, using different types for different workings."

After we spent a few minutes gazing, Michael was ready to begin the demonstrations.

"We'll begin by letting you experience the mirror as a gateway, so you can see the energy forms out there, and the energy fibers we talked about. I want you to gaze in your mirror and relax, listening as I take you on a guided visualization."

I placed my feet solidly on the floor and let my gaze drift off in an unfocused way. As I felt myself drifting into the mirror, I heard Michael's voice from far away giving me directions:

"Relax... Reach your meditative state of mind as you stare into the mirror... Let your eyes focus in and out as they will... Try to perceive the mirror as a surface you can look into... Think of it as a surface of water, having great depth... And now, picture yourself drifting into the mirror." Everything got dark and fuzzy now as he went on, "Merging with the darkness, come out in the air above your hotel... Look down, see the cars, the people, the lights and buildings... Go past all this and move down to the water... Go out over the water, and then, go under it... In that water, move on out into the ocean..."

I noticed it was getting cold as I reached the ocean's depths, and yet I also had the feeling of leaving my body very far behind. I was chilled in my mind, while my real body didn't exist. Far away, Michael's voice droned on.

"Now as you feel the coldness of the water around you, see the other individuals with you, and as we move through the water very fast, feel the currents... Notice the little luminous energies that are out there in the water floating around..."

I peered about, noticing a few of the long fibers of energies which Michael talked about, like octopus tendrils, with glowing lights at the end. They bobbed briefly in the water and then shot ahead like a school of fish. Michael was still speaking:

"Now, up ahead you may see some of the luminous energies are quite large, almost like jelly fish, and they seem to travel in schools, moving quickly through the water."

I followed them for awhile, and then Michael told me to come back. I resisted for a moment, wanting to continue floating with that energy school, but he went on, asking me to surface slowly, move back into the night air, and then slowly rise up into the clouds. From there, I came back to the mirror and into my body, relaxed, took a deep breath, and grounded myself under his directions. I felt a thud as I returned back in, and then emerging from the darkness, I saw my image in the mirror once more, fuzzy at first, but then more distinct. I felt that I had been away for a long time to a very far away place.

Michael then asked me to feel the surface of the mirror to notice a slight warm glow emanating from it. He said it was warm because I had created a gateway in it, and this was the energy raised from those activities. He asked me about the images I had seen, and I pointed out that they were clearer when he guided me, and that it was easier to stay with the experience. I wasn't distracted by other thoughts and images, or by an uncertainty about where I was going. He commented that this was because I had a clear objective, and suggested that taping myself guiding myself and then playing the tape back would help. Also, I would find that the more frequently I practiced, the more adept I would become, because I would be developing my own will and power, which would increase my focus and intention.

I asked if I should keep my eyes open or shut, and he thought it best to keep them opened, but out of focus. This way, the intention would stay focused on the mirror in front of me, even though the mirror might disappear while I was traveling on the other side of it.

Michael was ready for the next demonstration, which he called "working a gateway through a mirror." He set up his and Paul's mirror so they were facing each other on two chairs about ten feet apart. He put out the candles, so the room was in total darkness, except for the faint moonlight drifting in. He motioned for me to move closer to see the discharge of energy between his hand and the surface of his mirror. It flashed even more when he moved his hand. He asked me to move to the side out of the space between the two mirrors facing each other on the opposing chairs, while he activated it even more.

He held up his staff and stood slightly to the side. "Now, I'll visualize energy coming out of my power object and I'll make a working gateway in the glass." He moved his staff up and down a few times. "I'm visualizing this gateway projecting into the mirror, not into or through the glass, but into the working surface of the mirror itself, and from there, into its depths. It's going in through the energy of the mirror.

"Now, I'm picturing this gateway as a luminous depth into another dimension that just happens to have a reflective surface. And now I make the final incision, and you should notice a drop in the temperature in the room. Since the gateway is now open, the cooler air from the other dimension is rushing out." Then, he moved his hands in a tugging motion to widen the gateway. "We must watch this area in case something comes out, so that it can be controlled or sent back."

Michael asked me to watch the vibrations between the two mirrors, while he first sent through some energy, which evoked a slight breeze. Next he sent an energy dart through, while I noticed a brief glow flash and then fade away.

"Now, again notice the slight breeze coming from the area," he stated. "That's very important, because that breeze is part of a psychic coldness that exists in the mirror. Remember how we talked about that shadow middle world at that point where the cone tightens down into nothingness? Well, when you pass through the mirror, there's a similar point in space that's very cold, like outer space. It's as if you were traveling through a vacuum. The cold air is stronger when you use a mirror than with a regular gateway, because it's more focused. The breeze emanates from any disturbance of its cool air, such as your own energy passing into the gateway, and so the wind rushing out of the open gateway is a further confirmation of the existence of that gateway."

Then, Paul stepped out for his demonstration. Facing his mirror, he drew a slit with his own staff and widened it. At once, Greta and Sara commented that they could see the exchange of energy between the two mirrors like a series of laser beams. Michael informed us that they were observing this because the mirrors were linked, and the two energies were joined together in the center to become one stream of pulsating, vibrating energy flowing from one to the other and interacting. Michael put some more energy into this link while facing his own mirror, and the beams appeared brighter.

"What you are now seeing is a gate to gate connection. This connection is not limited to the ten feet we can see, but it could be as far away as miles, or even another universe because the gateways can link wherever they are."

Michael wanted to try something else. This time, he planned to shoot some energy into one mirror at an angle and have it hit the other mirror and reflect back out. He centered himself, breathed up some energy, created an energy dart, and pushed it out to the mirror.

"It seems like a burst of energy suddenly hitting the mirror," Greta exclaimed.

"I saw a little flash and then it ricocheted back," said Sara.

Michael did it a few more times. I asked how many times they could ricochet back.

"They can only go so far," he replied. "It depends on the intent of the person sending them. The process works like a triangle. The energy hits the first mirror, is shot from there almost instantaneously across space and hits the second mirror or another gateway where it is aimed, and then it returns into the gateway of the first mirror. The flash you see is created when it bounces off the second mirror and moves past the center point to the first gateway. This acts like a series of prisms reflecting energy, and you could set up any number of mirrors, but you would need to keep all the links clearly in mind throughout the whole process. If you miss just one link, the energy gets diverted and will miss its intended target. Starting with just two is best."

Next, he announced that he would send another dart and have it stop in the middle of the two mirrors. He asked us to observe it, but not to get so close that we were standing in the beam. We crowded around, and we all reported seeing a ball of luminous energy with sparkles and flashes at the midpoint. When Michael added more energy, we could see it glowing even more brightly. He invited us to look at it from various angles.

"You'll see it shooting back and forth now, and you might notice a lot of dark fibers shooting out along with the sparks as well. Also, you'll notice this energy beam is just in the physical area between the chairs. You could stand behind the chairs and not be harmed, but if you disturb the beam itself by getting too close this is dangerous. You would feel a disruption within your own aura, because you have passed into a strong energy field."

"The extent of this disruption would depend on the intention sent along with the energy, which usually will be minor," Paul added. "You want to be cautious whenever there's a strong concentration of energy somewhere, because you just don't know for sure what's there."

Then, Michael cut off the energy projection, so that the beam disappeared. He wanted to move on to the next demonstration.

"Now, you will see something even more amazing," he announced. "This time, you will see the energy activated by someone not even in the same room." He explained that he would go into another room and activate a mirror there. Then, he would project energy from this far away mirror into his own mirror here in the living room. Therefore, he pointed out, there is no need for a direct line between the mirrors. Just the will and intention alone is all that is needed for energy transfer.

But first, Paul had his own special demonstration before he shut down his own mirror. He wanted to project energy fibers out of his solar plexus into one gateway and have them come out through the other.

"But they won't go very far," he said. "Just around the chair."

I watched Paul standing in the darkness, facing Michael's mirror on the far side of the room. The room was quiet as he began to breathe deeply. Suddenly, I noticed a crackle of energy at Michael's mirror, and then Michael, who was standing next to Paul's mirror, announced:

"There, now he's at the surface of this mirror. You can see the bulging there. He's starting to reach through." And yes, I noticed the surface of Paul's mirror did look fuzzy to me.

"I can see it coming out of the mirror," Greta suddenly cried out.

"Yes," Michael nodded. "Like little tentacles coming out, and now you can see them reaching out. They're starting to stretch even more and cover the whole chair like a spider web."

"I have a sense of a plant growing over the chair," said Sara.

"Like an octopus," I observed. I saw what looked like a lumpy presence spilling out over the chair from the mirror.

"Yes, it's like that too," said Michael. "Also, there are some occasional sparkles and flashes. These are the energy discharges that are accompanying the projection."

Then, with a sucking motion, Paul slowly breathed the energy fibers back in.

"He has to do this one step at a time," Michael explained. "Just as he breathed out the energy to create these fibers, so he must gradually pull them back." Then, as Paul began to breathe more calmly and let his hands drop to his sides, Michael went on, "And now he is coming out of the mirror. If you watch, you can see the last bit of energy come out of the mirror as he grounds himself, so that the surface is quiet once more."

When Paul had brought himself out of concentration, he walked over and sealed his own mirror with some banishing motions. Michael headed for the other room to begin his demonstration and Paul indicated he would explain what was happening. We gathered around Michael's mirror to watch, and Paul began his explanation.

"Michael will be reaching through the mirror in the other room and into this mirror here." We all stared silently at the mirror and after about two minutes of quiet, Paul went on, "If you notice now, you can see him coming through here a few inches. You see the extra sparkles right about there, and then emerging from the area is a round, luminous shape. At the end, it expands again into a sharp, glowing tip, and you can see the fibers in the energy itself, although it's not solid.

"Now, notice he is withdrawing the energy. The form and color slowly dissolve as he breathes it back in. He must do it this way, since he has cut through to another dimension. This involves projecting a foreign substance into an alternate reality, so it's important to take it back in order to restore the original balance. It would be impolite not to. Also, this process is not like projecting energy into the ordinary universe, where it will ultimately dissipate."

Just then, Michael called out from the other room. "Okay. Here comes some more energy. I will send some darts through and go a little further with the energy this time."

Paul described what was happening. "Okay, that dart went almost to my mirror... Now that one came close to hitting the cabinet... That one's just hanging in the air... And that one hit the cabinet this time."

"Fine," Michael called out. "Now can you take them out for me?"

"Okay," Paul answered, moving about the room briskly and scooping up the energy forms with a whoosh of his hand. As he did this, I had to remind myself that everyone was talking about throwing energy. The conversation sounded so matter-of-fact, so mundane, that they could have been talking about softballs, not energy.

After Paul had located all the darts, Michael asked him to get rid of them, and Paul made his usual slashing and banishing motions to dispose of the old energy. Then, Michael announced that he would send some energy through in the form of his hand.

We watched Michael's mirror.

"Okay, I'll widen the gateway now," he called out from the other room. He paused for a moment. "Okay, and now it should be discharging."

Paul commented, "Notice the bubbling on the surface. It's starting to bulge from the energy discharge."

Michael called out that he was ready to send his hand, but first he wanted to remove his watch, or else that would mess up the circuitry. There was a long pause, and I could hear Michael breathing deeply from far away in the other room.

"This process takes a tremendous amount of energy," Paul observed.

Then suddenly, as we continued to watch, Paul cried out: "There, there. You can see it. The blackness in the middle of the bulging discharge. He's actually sticking his hand through the mirror, and it comes across black."

"Yes," Greta exclaimed. "It's like a black bar in the center."

Then, Michael announced he would spread his fingers, and Paul pointed out the aura that could be seen around them. Next Michael turned his hand sideways and again, Paul directed us to look at the changes in the mirror. He described seeing the discharge through Michael's palm.

Now, Michael was getting tired. He called out that he was pulling back because his hand was hurting him badly. I could hear him breathing in his energy in the other room, while Paul continued his commentary.

"There, you can see, as he pulls back, how the surface of the mirror is wrinkling a little around the side where it bulged up before. Eventually, that will smooth down. This process is like stretching a balloon, and now it's coming back to its normal size."

Greta wondered about the flashing, and Paul indicated this was due to the disruption of the surface. He said it would calm down when he sealed up the mirror, and he proceeded to do so.

Michael returned to the room, holding his hand as if it had been injured. "Now comes the healing process," he explained. "My hand is very drained, because it takes a lot of personal power to do what I just did. So I have to circulate some energy through it."

"How does your hand feel?" Greta asked. "And how long will it take to get it back to normal?"

"Well, it feels a little like my hand is not part of my body. It feels super cool, tingly, and numb. So it just needs a great deal of energy to come back to normal. Maybe just a few minutes of intense charge, and it will be fine."

"What would happen if you didn't do this?" I asked.

"Then the hand might develop problems," Michael answered. He shook his hand firmly and focused on sending energy to it. "But of course, the point is not to fail to do this, so these problems don't develop."

Then, as he nursed his hand, he explained what he had done in the other room. "First, I cut the gateway, and then, with a very focused intent, I created a full gateway in the mirror in the other room. Next I created an exit for that gateway into this mirror here. Finally, I put my hand into the gateway and focused on having the direct, living energy of my hand pass through the gateway to become visible in this mirror in the living room. Essentially, I was sending through the actual energy double of my hand. It is possible to do this with visualization. But that energy is an integral part of you, so it's like sending out your ghost or spirit." He had been cradling his hand, and now he breathed some more energy into it.

"Being able to do this is very significant, because it means it is possible for me to send forth a very concentrated energy in the form of my own image. I could send my whole image, and not just the hand, by raising more power to do so. I could project my own image or ghost through a mirror or a gateway anywhere. But it would take more visualization to come out of thin air, since it requires a very strong focus to create an exit point, and that is more difficult to do with empty air. So it's easier to come out of the mirror, since it's already there."

Next, Michael and Paul wanted to demonstrate the difference between using the surface of a mirror and the surface of water as a gateway. Michael brought out the black gazing bowl he had shown me earlier, but now it contained water. He lit a small candle so we could see better.

"I have already created a gateway into this bowl, and we will project energy into it." He walked over to his own mirror. "Now, I'll remove the seal from this, so it's re-energized again..." He made a few slashing marks in the air. "And now..." he turned to me, "...I'd like you to focus your attention on the bowl. I'll be projecting energy through the mirror to the charged bowl, and then charging the water." He concentrated, breathing deeply.

"There, you can already see the charge," Paul commented from his position near the bowl. "The water is rippling a little."

Michael continued to focus on the mirror and breathe. "Now I'll send energy out in the form of a visualized pentagram."

This time Paul reported seeing a bulge of energy about two inches above the surface, which gradually grew to about eight inches. "And now I see a kind of funnel dropping below it. It's like a white circle of energy floating on the water."

I gazed intently, but could only see a whitish, smoky haze.

"That's alright," Paul reassured me. "Everyone may see something a little different. I've been working with this for so long that I can see more distinctly. But the point is that you are seeing something. We all are. It just may take different forms."

They went on with the exercise. Now Michael went into the other room and again began projecting his hand through, much as he had tried earlier.

"I see a smoky cloud rising up," observed Sara.

"It's a little like a mushroom to me," Greta said.

"That's a pretty good description," Paul commented. "And now the form is growing more solid, though now he is spreading his fingers, and you can see the little darts of energy coming off of them."

Just then, Michael said, "Maybe now we can try to make contact," and Paul put his hand over the bowl. Slowly, he reached out into the smoky area we were all gazing at.

"Fingertip to fingertip," Michael said, and Paul extended his finger.

"Wow, I just saw a bright flash," Greta cried out.

Paul informed us that this was from the interaction of the energies. Then, they agreed to withdraw their hands and ended the exercise. Michael returned to the living room, and again needed to heal his right hand. He held it briefly over the bowl and breathed deeply. Greta handed him a small cup of water, and he held his hand over that. I wanted to know what he was doing.

"Again," Michael said, "the projection of my hand into the bowl took a lot of energy, so I'm replenishing some of this energy from the bowl. Also, before I started the exercise, I charged up the glass of water with my own energy. Using this glass now provides an especially strong dose of my own energy. Then, too, Greta gave me some of her energy as well, since she added her own charge to the water." He shook his arm vigorously. "Anyway, now I feel much better."

Paul sealed up the bowl, and Michael was ready to talk about the experience.

Michael asked me if I noticed any difference between the mirror and the water. I thought the water seemed more hazy, but I wasn't sure of anything.

But Michael seemed pleased. "Yes, that's exactly right. The image is more diffuse, because the water is a different medium than the mirror. It's more fluid, so the energy tends to diffuse, and it's even harder to project in a clear image. It's much easier in the mirror."

Then he spoke about the tremendous stress on the body required to do these activities. "You have to really put your whole will and intention into it, so you can project that energy of your double through. And I was just doing a projection of part of my body. So you can imagine how much stress there is to attempt to project the whole body through in a full gateway."

"Then why use these projections," I asked. "Why not just use something like conscious projection?"

"Because," Michael answered, "there's more reality in these energy projections. You are more sensitive and focused; what you see is more solid; and the experience is more powerful and intense. It's like the difference between seeing slides of London or actually being there."

Still nursing his arm, he also pointed out that these demonstrations tonight had taken more energy than usual, because he was focusing on not only projecting his energy, but also on making the result visible to us. He was employing a visual focus besides the usual focus on energy projection alone. He indicated that so far he had been able to project a full shoulder, and was working on doing a full body projection soon.

Just then, he noticed his watch on the table. "Incidentally," he added, "you should be careful with electronic things when you try anything psychic. For example, the silicon chips in the watch are especially vulnerable to damage if they pass through these energy fields. When I forget to remove electronic devices, their circuitry gets all haywire, and I can't repair it."

Finally, Michael had one last suggestion. "It's also possible to send a familiar through to any location to do almost any task you want, instead of going yourself. This is advanced stuff, but you will want to keep it in mind. It can save you an extra expenditure of energy, like having an employee to work for you."

And on that note, he suggested we take a quick break. He wanted to show me one more technique with mirrors, this one for raising energy. "You will need to replenish your own energy, too, because you will need lots of it tonight when you attempt your gateway."

# CHAPTER FIFTEEN

## *GOING THROUGH A GATEWAY*

After our brief break for coffee and cookies in the kitchen, we returned to get back to work. I put on my heavy, black down jacket, and black Russian hat I had brought, so I would be completely in black for the working, and I joined Michael, Paul, Greta, and Sara outside on the patio. As Michael had instructed, I brought my mirror along with me.

"Now," Michael said, holding up his own mirror to demonstrate, "what I'll be doing is charging this mirror up again to make it receptive. Then, you can do the same with your own mirror."

He moved his free right hand across the mirror in a triangular motion. "I'm projecting energy out of my hand as I draw an upwards pointing triangle. Then, I'm charging it to create a receptive triangle to draw in the energy of the moon. And now..." Michael gazed into the mirror and breathed in deeply, "I'm pointing the mirror so the moon is reflected in it, and I'm breathing in the energy of the moonlight which is reflected in the glass. At the same time, I'm doing the seeing exercises on the moon."

He asked me to do the same. As he instructed I drew the upwards receptive triangle, projecting energy out of my hand as I drew it, and then I concentrated on having the intention that this triangle would be receptive to the energy it received. Next, I positioned the mirror so I could see the moon in it, and with my free hand, I pulled the energy of the moon down, visualizing it hitting the mirror's surface and charging it. I breathed in the energy of the moonlight through the triangle, doing my seeing exercise at the same time. As I stood there breathing in for a few minutes, I could feel a kind of glow of energy radiate through my body as I did this. I felt more alive and alert.

Michael asked me if I felt more energized, and I nodded.

"Good," he said. "The moon energy usually does that. In fact, if you look at your aura in the mirror now, you may see that something has happened.

I noticed a fuzzy glow around my reflection.

"It seems like it's a little brighter and larger," I said.

"That's right. You have more energy. Also, you can use this mirror for divination with the technique I just showed you tonight, though we won't do that now. Using it for divination, you would ask a question as you pull the moonlight in. Then, feel the answer. But be careful of what you ask, because moonlight is very truthful. Be sure it's an answer you are prepared to learn."

Then, we were done with the energy raising exercise for the night. I drew a sealing pentagram to seal the mirror, and closed it up for the night. We all went inside.

"So now you should be ready to try your gateway," Michael stated.

"I hope so," I said.

"Don't hope," he responded. "You must have a firm intent. You must feel confident you can do it. You must believe."

"Okay then, I'm ready," I replied, and I went to my car outside to get my staff. I joined them in the kitchen, and when we were all ready, we headed out to the cars to drive to a park high up in the canyons above Beverly Hills. On the way, Michael tried to reassure me about what would happen and give me some last minute reminders. I still held some doubts about whether I believed enough to accomplish the task ahead. I felt nervous about this seemingly critical test of ability which I had to perform in front of everyone.

"Paul will do a demonstration of what you are going to do," he explained, "and then I'll review the directions with you. Then you will have your chance. You should be fully prepared, but remember that your ability to do this depends on your visualization and focus. In order to go through the gateway, you have to believe. If you question it, it will break the energy dynamic. You must be receptive, and your visualization must be good."

I nodded, understanding, yet still feeling uncertain I could do all that was required.

We drove up the winding canyon road high in the hills, with Paul's truck just behind us. Michael continued:

"Let me tell you briefly what to expect when you go out there. You will see a lot of fog around you, and maybe the edges of the gateway. More than anything, you will feel the gateway, especially the point at which you enter another reality. You'll just feel this void, and then you'll enter it, and everything will feel different inside, so you'll know.

"Meanwhile, we will stand nearby. If anything untoward happens, we'll be ready to intercede and help."

We drove a few more miles, and I could see the lights from the valley twinkling below, reminding me of the reality I would try to leave.

"Remember, we expect you to cut the gateway, then see it or feel it, walk to the edge of it, and then put some energy out so you can reach into it and penetrate it yourself to see what's inside. And then return. It's a simple process, but you must focus and believe. As you will see for yourself, there are certain physical things that indicate you have come to the edge, and you will know you have been successful." And with that, we finished the last few minutes of driving along some narrow roads to the park.

We got out of our cars and proceeded to hike up a winding dirt road that wound around a wooded hillside to our left. As we climbed higher, there were rolling hills to our right, with their tops shrouded in fog, and far in the distance, the lights of the valley. After about ten minutes, we came to a high, flat area overlooking the valley. Michael sent Paul and Greta to check out two connecting dirt roads to this spot where we would be working to be sure everything was clear ahead. We needed to be certain we would not be interrupted in our work.

I glanced back along the road we had come in on. It looked dark and desolate, shadowed by the trees. Just the journey alone helped me to feel that we had indeed moved to some extent out of ordinary reality into this isolated mountain spot. I was already starting to feel somewhat removed in space and time.

After a few minutes, Paul returned, and while we waited for Greta to finish her scouting, Paul explained what he would be doing in his demonstration.

"I'll be starting with an energy raising exercise to bring the energy up," he began. "Then, I'll draw a circle around myself and select the spot where I want the gateway." He pointed to the grassy knoll in the center where the three roadways came together. "I'll cut the gateway about twenty feet out. Once I have created it, I will reach out with my will to create a line to it and through it. Then, I will visualize the opening of the gateway as I look into another dimension. Following the line I sent out to the gateway, I'll walk there very slowly, and then go in."

He stepped forward a few paces to indicate the slow, lumbering gate he would use. "Now, when you walk out there," he advised me, "you want to bring the energy around you, as if you are cutting through a fog that you draw to yourself. As you walk, visualize that fog growing thicker and thicker. When you reach the limits of the gateway, where it goes off into nothing, stop and stand there for awhile and feel it. Then, try to reach through it a little. You can look in with your vision alone, by seeing a line going out into the gateway in your mind's eye. Or, you can extend the luminous fibers from your solar plexus to pull you inside, and you can use them to feel around in there, if you feel comfortable doing that. Then, back out, and walk back through the fog down the line you have drawn to the circle. When you return to the circle, close the gateway, draw the energy line back in, and take down the circle. You may need help with this final part, but we'll be here to help you."

Just then, Greta returned, and Paul went out to do his demonstration. He stepped out to the area he had indicated, a shadowy figure in the dim moonlight, who I could barely make out. Michael stood beside me making occasional comments. "Okay, now he's raising his energy... Now he's making his circle... He's creating a gateway..."

Meanwhile, I watched intently. I noticed a gradually growing, yellow aura emerge around Paul, becoming ever stronger as I watched, and then a slight glimmer of a fuzzy line extended out about twenty feet in front of him. Soon, I could see a fuzzy, foggy area in front of him, with a slight indentation or rippling in the center.

"That's his gateway," Michael observed when I described what I was seeing, "and now, if you look at his stomach, you can see how he's extending some luminous fibers. They are growing and reaching out into the gateway."

Paul began to walk slowly towards the gateway. It seemed as if he was being pulled towards it, and Michael explained that it was the fibers pulling him in. "Look closely, and you can see that they are latched onto something in there, and he is reeling himself in with those fibers. And look..." he pointed to what appeared like a mass of energy behind Paul, "there's a silver cord behind him which is attached to his circle. He may use that cord to help him get back in, although you don't always need that. You can just follow the line you create."

I nodded, and we continued to watch for a few minutes as Paul stood in the gateway he had created. He seemed to fade in and out of my vision as I watched, and it almost looked like some curtain of fog was slipping up and down between him and us separating our two worlds of different realities—the world on the other side of the gateway and our world outside.

And then Paul was on his way back, and I could see him again as a shadowy silhouette against the distant hills. As he stood quietly meditating in his circle, and then started banishing motions in the air, Michael continued, "And now he's pulling in his energy... He's closing the gateway and taking down his circle."

Finally, the demonstration completed, Paul returned to our group. Briefly, Michael commended him for his strong visual performance, especially his display of the luminescent fibers. Then, once again, they both reviewed with me what I should do. By this time, we had been over the procedure so many times, that I felt I didn't have to think about it.

"So now, if you're ready," Michael finished, "you can begin."

I walked slowly out to the center of the plateau area, suddenly feeling very self-conscious. I pushed away my feelings and concentrated on the task at hand, keeping my focus and intent in mind.

In the center of the area, I stopped and gazed down at the ground to get centered. I remembered the energy exercise I had first learned, of breathing in energy of different colors through my chakras, and I began doing this. I started to feel calmer, and the group watching me seemed to recede into the background, while the vastness of the area around me stretched out to the sky, almost as if into infinity. I felt a tremendous sense of isolation, and being vulnerable and alone. Just me and the elements of nature around me; the land, the sky, the valley below, and nothing else.

As a gust of wind blew, I took a deep breath, and holding my staff towards the ground, I began to make my circle, moving my staff slowly in a clockwise direction as I turned with it. Next, looking about twenty feet ahead, I lifted my staff and brought it down several times to make the slit to form the gateway, and after that I moved my hands back and forth in a rolling motion to widen it, as Michael had taught me. I imagined there was a line of energy connecting my circle and this gateway I had created, and I began to walk slowly along this.

I concentrated on the images of the circle, line, and gateway as I moved. Reflecting on them, I noticed, helped to make them real. At least I could feel and see, if ever so faintly, the forms which I had visualized in my mind's eye, and it appeared as if they had taken on a visual or physical reality in front of me as I concentrated.

I stopped before what I imagined was the gateway. I experienced it as a wall of energy in front of me with a small slit in it, but as I stood there, I began to question the reality of it. Was this real? Could I step through? Or was I just imagining all this? I lifted my staff hesitantly, as if I was waiting for the right moment to step in. At the same time, I felt as if my visualization was starting to crumble with the questions forming in my mind.

Off to my left I heard a voice. Was someone coming? I wondered what to do, and then I recognized Michael's voice, and I heard him tell me to make the gateway a little wider. This was all the reassurance I needed, for at least one other person was sharing the same reality I was trying to create.

With renewed resolve, I lifted my staff and made another slit in the wall of energy I now saw as a more solid form in front of me. I widened the slit, using the same rolling motions I had before. But this time my motions were firmer, surer, my intention more focused.

"Okay, that's better now," I heard Michael saying. "You can enter the gateway now."

I took a few steps forward. Remembering Paul's demonstration of energy fibers, I imagined some fibers projecting out of my solar plexus and into the gateway to help pull me in. After I imagined them latching onto something behind the gateway opening, I followed their pull and very slowly walked in.

At once, everything seemed very foggy. I looked off in the distance, and now there seemed to be a curtain of haze between me and the valley below. I started to turn my head to the left and to the right, and felt almost afraid to look, as if the slightest movement might disrupt my concentration and start the walls of the gateway crumbling again. As I tried to focus on the haziness in front of me, I saw what appeared to be sparkles of energy. Then, off to my right, from the hillside, I heard Michael and Paul calling to me.

"Look around at us," Michael was saying.

"Tell us what you see," said Paul. "What do we look like?"

Slowly, cautiously, I turned so as not to break the trancelike mood, and then I tried to tell them what I saw. "I don't know. Fuzzy, foggy. You seem far away." I felt uncertain, hesitant. What should I be seeing? I started to feel tired, spacey.

Then I heard Michael saying: "Yeah, we should be foggy and far away, because you're seeing us through a gateway. You're in another dimension, so it's like seeing through a misty glass. So now, I'd like you to back out of your gateway. Let yourself out slowly, and come back into ordinary reality."

I turned and faced the valley again. Slowly I stepped backwards, through the opening, and as I did, I felt the energy fibers I had sent out suddenly evaporate, and in moments, the area in front of me suddenly appeared clear again, and I could see the lights shining brightly. I felt a little tired and dazed, as if I had been in a long day dream.

As I slowly backed up, I could see Greta and Paul out of the corner of my eye running around and jumping up and down, making slashing motions in the sky, although I didn't understand exactly what they were doing.

"Now, just wait there for a little bit," Michael told me.

I waited quietly, feeling the vibrancy of the plain around me, as the wind blew across it. Everything seemed so sparkly, so alive, as if I was seeing it for the first time, and the lights from the valley seemed even bigger and brighter than before. Meanwhile, as I waited, I could hear the crackle of leaves under their feet, as Greta and Paul jumped around. Finally, they were finished doing whatever they were doing, and Michael told me to close my gateway and turn around to return to the circle.

I made a few banishing motions to seal the gateway up, turned, and walked back. I followed the line of energy I had originally drawn, but it was very hard to see now. The experience was over, and I seemed to be left with only my memory of it. I stopped where I remembered my circle to be, but Michael asked me to walk ahead a few more feet, because I had missed it. When I was back in the circle, he instructed me to take it down. I retraced the circle I had drawn in the opposite direction, counterclockwise, and returned to the group. I felt unsure again—had I passed the test?

But Michael and Paul wanted to ask me some questions first. What did I experience? What did I see and feel?

I described how I cut the gateway and walked out to it. I mentioned how I tried to visualize energy fibers going out and pulling me in; how things appeared foggy when I passed through; how I felt spacey and isolated when I was inside.

They looked thoughtful. I still wasn't sure if I had passed, and I was hesitant to ask. So I asked them what they had seen, as a way of confirming that what had happened had been real.

Paul replied first. He began slowly, recalling, "I saw you draw a nice solid circle. When you reached out with your power object, the tip looked a little fuzzy at first, but then the energy you were sending out became sharper with use. As you opened the gateway, a cloudy formation appeared, and as you moved closer to it, this cloud seemed to envelop you. When you crossed the threshold, the foggy curtain closed in around you, and after this, I could mainly see a double of your aura behind you, which looked like a being of about two times your size, and golden in color. Then I noticed a dark brooding figure over your left shoulder that made me anxious."

"A dark, brooding figure?" I asked, surprised.

"Well, don't worry about it," he went on. "We got rid of it later, while you were standing in front of the gateway after you came out." I remembered the slashing motions Paul and Greta had been doing, and all the running around.

"While you were inside," he continued, "I saw you moving around a little, and as you came back out, it was as if the atmosphere of the other world was dropping off away from you. When you sealed up the gateway, you closed up most of this energy, but there were still some smaller stray energy forms left hanging outside. You weren't aware of them, so Greta and I stepped in and cleaned them up, and we sent them back by banishing them. We opened up our own partial gateways, and then pushed them back in. Though we had to chase around a few of them. Like that dark being behind you; he could run very fast. But I finally cornered him, and sent him back."

"I didn't see any of that," I said wonderingly.

"No, you were focused on your intent to get back to your circle, so you weren't paying any attention. Besides, usually your first time you usually need some help to close your gateway and chase anything you bring back through. So we were ready and waiting, and that's what we did."

Then Michael described his own observations, most of them echoing what Paul had observed, though he added some details. "First, I saw you raising your energy, and gradually, a luminous blue energy gathered around you like a flame. As you created your circle, it was like a shock wave of energy rising, and with the creation of the gateway, I saw changes in the air. It was as if you had created a fold in the atmosphere, and from this, a fogginess developed. The air around you became wispy.

"But I noticed that your gateway was too small at first. You needed more width for your body, so I came over to remind you. As I walked around you, I saw your gateway a little ways ahead. It had a luminous gray lip, and emanating from this, a yellowish-white tunnel. When you walked in, the yellow fog gathered around you, and it appeared as if you has passed through a veil. Then you became fuzzy, and the further you walked in, the fuzzier you got.

"You also seemed to move much more slowly, and there was a definite feeling of isolation from you. I felt as if I was talking to you through a plate of glass, and as I approached, I sensed a wall of energy on both sides. It's hard to describe—an electrical feeling, a nervous sensation. But there was definitely a sense of an energy barrier, so I stayed clear of it.

"Like Paul, I saw the other beings nearby. I left Paul and Greta to deal with them. When you started to back out of your gateway, you became clearer, and once you were fully back into your circle, you appeared normal. Your normally high energy was back."

Greta and Sara agreed they had seen pretty much the same things. I finally asked if I had passed.

"Yes, yes," Michael smiled at me. "It was a good gateway for the first time. We don't expect perfection. You were able to perform the key things we were looking for. Your visualization was good, and we were able to see the outcome of it—your visualization of the gateway and that envelope of fog around it. Also, for a few minutes, you penetrated the border between the two realities, and that is why you felt so isolated, and why we seemed so far away. But for now, your gateway was strong and clear enough. So, congratulations. You passed the grade."

Then, to symbolize this, Michael took a small silver box with two sets of double stars out of his pocket. He put them on the tips of my shirt collar in place of the single silver stars that were already there. "Congratulations," he repeated. "You've now passed your fifth degree."

After some quick handshakes and congratulations from the others, we walked back down the path to our cars. On the way back, the hills, the trees, the stars, the very air around us seemed more vibrant, more alive. It was as if there was a glow in the air now, and as I reflected on my experience, I thought about how it all seemed a little unreal. I wasn't sure I could ever know the truth. Had I really been able to step into an alternate reality, or did I just imagine I had? And did the others really see me do this or imagine I did, too? But then, it sounded like the woods and wind around us were calling to me, and from far away I heard an owl hooting, and it sounded as if it were saying over and over, "Believe, believe."

As we drove back, Michael had a few things to add about gateways. "The point of making and entering a gateway," he told me, "is to provide us a door to anywhere. We can project our will or consciousness anywhere we wish. We can travel to distant places in this world or just observe what is there, and we can work with spirits or bring in things from other dimensions, such as helpful forms and familiars. The basic key to all this is the ability to cut the gateway and to experience the entryway, as you have done. This takes real focus and energy, and if you want to go further, you can enter another dimension fully. Tonight you were gazing out from the border between two worlds, but you had not entered the other world completely. What determines where you are is your will and focused visualization. So you were no longer in ordinary reality or fully in an alternate one, but right in the middle. And being in this middle place is unique, because the rules of either world don't apply.

"It's like being in a area where there are no rules; out of space and time. For the shaman, this elastic state is ideal, because you can create your own rules. You can do more with your will, because there is less to hamper you. You can go either way from this zero point or void. Back to ordinary reality or on to other worlds. So, while you remain in the middle, your will, your intention, your consciousness can roam free. There are no barriers. You can do what you want by suspending your doubts and developing your power of visualization. You have to be able to see and to believe. You have to be able to believe and see."

See and believe. The words echoed through my mind as we continued down the canyon. And then Michael interrupted my reflection on all that had happened.

"Well, now that you've passed your grade, we can start your advanced training tomorrow. We'll be doing some more advanced work with energy, and we'll be working with familiars and spirits. Now that you can make a gateway, you will be able to travel through it and call on the spirits and energy forms from the other side to help you in everyday life. You'll also learn how to call on and work with your own familiar—a personal spirit or form who is bound to you, like a friend you can call on when you need extra help. So there will be much to do."

I nodded. "Okay," I said, as Michael pulled into his driveway and stopped the car. "I'll see you tomorrow."

Then, after I waved goodbye to Paul, Greta, and Sara, I got into my own car and drove away. The words, "see and believe," continued to echo in my mind as I made my way down the narrow canyon road. As I came to the bottom, I noticed a heavy, rolling fog that seemed like a curtain across the road. As I plunged slowly into it, I felt I was entering another gateway, and I headed back to my hotel in the foggy night.

## ABOUT THE AUTHOR

You can contact Gini Graham Scott, Ph.D., J.D. regarding workshops, seminars, speaking engagements and books on shamanism, personal success, creativity and other topics at:

CHANGEMAKERS
715 48th Avenue
San Francisco, CA 94121
(415) 387-1771

Besides *Secrets of the Shaman,* Dr. Scott is the author of three other books on shamanism—*Shaman Warrior* (published by New Falcon Publications), *Shamanism and Personal Mastery,* and *Shamanism For Everyone.* Her next book on shamanism, which features her continued work with the master shaman described in *Secrets of the Shaman,* will be *Shaman Initiation.* Her books on personal success and creativity include: *The Empowered Mind, Mind Power: Picture Your Way to Success, Resolving Conflict* and *The Creative Traveler.*

She has published over twenty books on various topics and has appeared on the Phil Donahue, Sally Jesse Raphael and Jerry Springer shows. She has a weekly radio talk show series—CHANGEMAKERS—featuring interviews on various topics. The program airs in 70 countries.

Dr. Scott received her Ph.D. from the University of California at Berkeley in Sociology, and has a J.D. from the University of San Francisco Law School.